INDICTMENT

&

APPLICATION/PETITION FOR A PUBLIC ENQUIRY

INTO STATE-SPONSORED CRIMINALITY IN IRELAND

&

The case for the establishment of the Peoples Tribunal of Ireland according to the Rule of Law

INDICTMENT
& APPLICATION-PETITION FOR A PUBLIC ENQUIRY
Into State-Sponsored Criminality in Ireland
ISBN-13: 978-1-906628-93-2
Published by CheckPoint Press, Ireland.

www.checkpointpress.com

This book is available worldwide as a POD title online – or from
your local bookshop by quoting the ISBN from the rear cover.
It has been priced so as to be affordable for all.

Bulk orders (of 10+ copies) may be sourced at 10% discount
directly from 'bookstore@checkpointpress.com'.

AUTHOR'S PREFACE

"THERE ARE MECHANISMS IN PLACE" (they tell us) by which we are supposed to be able to guarantee the Rule of Law in this State - which is how and why we remain members of the United Nations, the Council of Europe and the EU. But these mechanisms depend on honest people doing their jobs. Police, lawyers, senior civil servants, judges, TD's, Ministers - and even the President too, all have the power and the responsibility to ensure the Rule of Law and the protection of our fundamental rights. Unfortunately, there are far too many 'shady incentives' to protect those in power - no matter how corrupt or dysfunctional they may be - and if there's one thing the modern Irish State has become expert at - it is the active facilitation and cover-ups of political, white-collar and regulatory crime. In fact, we could very well be the world leaders in those dark arts by now, and all the while, the *pretence* of Irish democracy and accountability is paraded on the world stage with cunningly-disarming, 'diddle-dee-dee' Irish charm.

This small booklet is a serious, damning indictment of the toxic culture that permeates the Irish political and legal world. It asks and demands that the Irish Government abides by the Rule of Law by first of all acknowledging the multiple documented proofs of serious, criminal wrongdoing by senior officials and office holders who continue to act with brass-necked impunity and contempt for the law, for the Constitution and for our fundamental human rights. The law requires that these people are either reformed, or replaced; gone/sacked/fined/imprisoned - or whatever will ensure the frauds,

3

the deceptions, the corruption, the thefts of land, of public resources and monies, the bribery and brown envelopes, the perjuries, the lies and forgeries, the frame-ups and targeting of otherwise decent people, the conspiracies and rampant rule breaking in the Courts... that all of this shameful, disreputable activity stops right now! The Government is obliged by law to act on this application for a Public Enquiry. Whether they will or not, will probably all come down to what they think they can get away with while the public is distracted elsewhere. The very fact that they can dismiss outright any complaints or applications that actually NAME any alleged offender should be warning enough. Over 10 years of systemic stonewalling should seal the deal! If we are to live in an autocratic regime where the Rule of Law only applies only to those of us who are gullible enough or complicit enough to never raise a dissenting voice, then we really need to start thinking of our childrens' futures, and of all those who came before us who suffered and died for a better world. Who are we to just give it all away to a shower of career miscreants and moral deviants? This book contains our arguments for why the Irish State - and particularly the Irish Courts are operating unlawfully and immorally with the full knowledge and complicity of the establishment. It shows how the Rule of Law has effectively been replaced by a fog of misdirection and political deceit, and why we urgently need some honest Courts that do not operate as commercial franchises with the common agenda of protecting the status quo. This little book also details the arguments and legal reasonings for the setting up of the Peoples Tribunal, and how it will serve the Irish public.

IMPORTANT FOREWORD

THIS PUBLICATION IS AN AMALGAMATION OF; (i) the formal Petition Statement that was prepared for submission to the Joint Petitions Committee (JPC) of the Houses of the Oireachtas under the terms of *the 2013 Act*, plus (ii) the formal Declaration that was served 'under seal' on various offices of the State pertaining to the necessary lawful establishment, on July 1st 2020, of *The Peoples Tribunal of Ireland*.

In pursuit of these objectives, various versions of the *Integrity Ireland Report, "Criminality in the Irish Courts"* were produced. The 1st 62-page pdf version was served on the Irish authorities on January 13th & 14th 2020. The 2nd 98-page version was served again on various State Offices in May, June and July 2020. Failing any due acknowledgements or responses, the 3rd 270-page version entitled, *"Criminality in the Irish Courts – and the absence of the Rule of Law"* was published in July 2020, ISBN 978-1-906628-888.

One of the first listed criteria for the submission of a Petition to the JPC is that it, *"does not contain the name or names of individuals"*. Accordingly, a 4th 50-page amended and redacted 'JPC Version' of the original I-I Report was created. On July 29th, the day before the Government took its annual break, the Secretariat to the JPC advised us that, *"no petitions could be accepted at this time as the previous Committee had been disbanded on January 14th"* and they had, *"no information about when the new committee will be up and running."* We served that 50-page Report on the JPC Offices on July 31st 2020.

A PETITION

To the Houses of the Oireachtas

&

The Joint Committee on Public Petitions & the Justice Committee

&

To qualified, interested parties

Concerning certain matters of general public concern and/or interest in relation to the legislative powers of the Houses of the Oireachtas concerning issues of public policy

Noting that: *"The establishment of the petitions system will enable greater citizen interaction with the parliamentary system on matters of general public concern or interest. Only one signature is needed to submit a petition. This parliamentary petitions system presents an important avenue for individuals to participate in the democratic process, through the petitions process. Members of the public are able to take their policy concerns directly to the heart of Parliament and to influence the parliamentary agenda."*

Oireachtas online, July 2020

CONTENTS

*   *   *

THIS PUBLICATION INCLUDES AN APPLICATION TO INVESTIGATE, IMPEACH, and/or REMOVE FROM OFFICE CERTAIN OFFICIALS & OFFICE HOLDERS OF THE IRISH STATE

Under the terms of the Houses of the Oireachtas (Inquiries, Privileges and Procedures) Act 2013

- and -

A FORMAL DECLARATION AS SERVED 'UNDER SEAL' ON VARIOUS OFFICES OF STATE AND OTHER INTERESTED PARTIES PERTAINING TO THE URGENT AND NECESSARY ESTABLISHMENT OF THE PEOPLES TRIBUNAL OF IRELAND IN ACCORDANCE WITH THE RULE OF LAW

As sent 'under seal' to the President of Ireland and the Council of State; 'cc' senior officials and office holders in the Irish State, July 2020. Copies to the UN, the CoE and the European Union.

8

INTRODUCTION

The sovereignty and legitimacy of any State is defined by—and is dependent upon—that State's adherence to 'a rule of law' by which the government asserts and maintains its authority. In the case of member States of the United Nations, of the Council of Europe and of the European Union, membership of these bodies is dependent not merely upon the fact (or claim) that there is '*a* rule of law' or that 'rule *by* law' exists in that State, but upon each Member States' declared respect for, and statutory application of, "*the* Rule of Law" and the parallel values of democracy, human rights, social justice and economic freedom which combined concepts underpin the collective political morality of those said institutions.

**THE UNIVERSAL PRINCIPLES
OF THE RULE OF LAW**

That the government as well as private actors are accountable under the law. That the laws are clear, publicized, and stable; that they are applied evenly; and that they protect fundamental rights, including the security of persons and contract, of property, and of human rights.

Consequently, if it can be shown that any Member State of the UN, the CoE or the EU does NOT respect or abide by the Rule of Law – or indeed that there exists a chronic and systemic failure (or refusal) to even properly maintain any consistent rule *of* law or rule *by* law – then clearly that State is suffering a crisis of sovereignty and statutory legitimacy sufficient to challenge its continued membership of those institutions, at least until such time as the Rule of Law is properly re-established and is being fully and effectively applied.

The primary purpose of this Publication is to place 'on the record' in one concise document:

(i)   The requirement that the Irish Government establishes without delay a *Part 2 Enquiry* under the terms of *the Houses of the Oireachtas (Inquiries, Privileges and Procedures) Act 2013* as referenced herein, and upon the factual contents and commentary contained in the 50-page 'JPC Version' of the I-I Report entitled, *"CRIMINALITY IN THE IRISH COURTS – A Provisional Report by the Integrity Ireland Association" [PDF attached].*

(ii) To provide to the UN General Assembly, the Council of Europe and the EU Commission the materials necessary to take the appropriate action to ensure that the Irish State returns to a position of full and proper compliance with the Rule of Law, and by association, with its sworn obligations under UN, CoE and EU membership, or, to endure the prescribed consequences of failing to do so.

(iii) To articulate the legal grounds and conditions upon which *The Peoples' Tribunal of Ireland* has been lawfully and necessarily established.

1. ABSENCE OF THE RULE OF LAW IN IRELAND

We respectfully draw your attention to the original 62-page PDF I-I Report entitled, *"Criminality in the Irish Courts - A Provisional Report by the Integrity Ireland Association, Part One"*. This 'I-I Report' document was served on all Irish authorities including all sitting TD's and Senators of the 32nd Dáil on January 13th & 14th 2020. It contained lists of documented crimes against domestic and international law that are being committed with licence and impunity by Irish officials and office holders. The accused were not specifically named in that Report but their respective offices, titles and positions were. The recipients of that Report were invited to simply return to us for the names of the accused – which would be forwarded to them by email, freely and without delay. None of the listed recipients did so.

The Report was then forwarded to the Petitions Committee of the European Parliament – which in turn drew some curious and unexpected responses which arguably amount to an unqualified attempt to block admissibility of that I-I Report and any further correspondence on the matter. References to the text of the accompanying EU Petition were subsequently removed from the EUPC website.

In anticipation of *some* official response from *some* quarter, and in order to provide the substantive evidence, a full 270-page (black) Report comprising Parts One & Two was published under the title,

"Criminality in the Irish Courts – and the absence of the Rule of Law" [ISBN: 978-1-906628-88-8] which the author makes available, at cost, to any official body who is conducting an investigation. A condensed 98-page PDF (blue) version of that full Report was served again on July 3rd 2020 on President Higgins and on various named members of the newly-formed government, but again, without any responses or acknowledgements. In addition to the publication of the *PTI Operations Manual* [ISBN: 978-1906628-91-8] those two follow-up versions of the 1st I-I Report contain additional proofs and evidence in support of the overall theme; that there is a crisis of endemic and systemic criminality embedded in the institutions of the Irish State and a consequent, parallel, absence of the Rule of Law in any credible, consistent form.

In July 2020 a 4th (green) amended-and-redacted 50-page version of the original I-I Report (which is now absent the names of any persons other than the Petitioner) was compiled in order to meet the criteria for a submission to the Joint Petitions Committee of the Houses of the Oireachtas, and it is chiefly upon that latter document that our Formal Application for a Public Enquiry by the Irish State is grounded under the terms of *the Houses of the Oireachtas (Inquiries, Privileges and Procedures) Act 2013,* and according to the respective admissibility criteria as quoted on the Oireachtas website.

Scope of the Report: Of necessity, the pilot I-I Report deals with a succession of interconnected events experienced by just one individual and his family over a period of several years. Other cases known to the *Integrity Ireland Association* with comparable identifiers – some of which include several of the named accused as well as other repeat offenders – were not included in the launch publication due to the necessity to have just one source of authorship; one locus for confirmations; and just one target for anticipated reprisals by the establishment including any disreputable attempts to suppress, deny, or denounce the contents – and/or to discredit and vilify the author – such as in the cases of Sgt Maurice McCabe and other outspoken whistleblowers, reporters and activists.

Summary: The I-I Report documents the disturbing fact that we have, over a period of several years now, made all manner of lawful approaches – both formal and informal – to the Irish statutory authorities and to other agencies and oversight bodies; to address numerous documented incidences of unlawful and unconstitutional behaviour including serious, repeat, criminal activities by persons in the employ of the Irish State (and/or in the pay of the State, or otherwise affiliated with the State) noting that the persistence and frequency of the said illicit behaviour and the corresponding failures and refusals of the respective authorities to deal with prohibited conduct according to the law has resulted in the alarming circumstances where the requisite 'Rule of Law' is not in effect being respected, applied or adhered to in any recognisably-consistent or equitable manner sufficient to qualify the Irish State as having, *"a properly functioning justice system"* complete with, *"competent, lawfully-established domestic Courts with effective appeal mechanisms"* that are overseen by, *"a politically-independent judiciary who abide by the law"*; such as is required under the Irish Constitution and which said national political status is mandatory for membership of; (a) the European Union, (b) the Council of Europe, and (c) the United Nations.

Methodology & Evidence: For the avoidance of any doubt; our lawful approaches to the statutory authorities over a 10+ year period are detailed in numerous letters, formal complaints and in affidavits on the public record in the Superior Courts, and include (but are not limited to) the following:

- Lodging criminal complaints with An Garda Síochána and Garda HQ (Irish police).

- Lodging formal complaints to internal authorities within each agency or affiliate business, including to: the Law Society; the Bar Council; the CEO of the Courts Service; An Post; HSE/TUSLA; the DPP's Office; to various Ministers of State; to the named Presidents of the Courts; the respective Taoisigh; and to the Offices of the President of Ireland.

- Seeking support and assistance and initiating follow-up complaints and enquiries with the respective 'Statutory Oversight Bodies' including to the Minister for Justice; the Garda Commissioner; the Ombudsman; the

Information Commissioner; the Garda Síochána Ombudsman Commission; the Chief of Staff of the Defence Forces; the Irish Human Rights Commission; the Department of Justice Review Panel; the DPP, and the Charleton Tribunal.

- Contacting ALL of the firms of solicitors listed on the Criminal legal Aid Panel and making direct contact with 1,874 Irish Barristers for the purposes of seeking legal representation.

- Pursuing private civil and criminal actions in the Courts.

- Lodging numerous applications and appeals to the Superior Courts.

- Making formal applications to the European Court of Human Rights.

- Writing to all sitting TD's, Ministers of State and sitting Judges.

- Lodging a petition to the European Parliament.

- Sending, offering, or making available to all of the said parties, physical evidence and other unchallengeable proofs of alleged criminality.

- Initiating valid citizens' arrests of a number of officials and office holders.

- Making dozens of valid applications for criminal summonses under *S.10 of the Petty Sessions Act,* and, when unlawfully refused, rejected or ignored, and/or when refused entry to the Courts by gardaí; by following up via alternative lawful processes such as here listed.

- Setting up the *Integrity Ireland Association* in support of victims and survivors of State-sponsored illegalities, and to lobby the Irish authorities for civil justice and political reform.

- Placing a series of formal 'QTC' Notices & Declarations on the record for the purposes of legal clarity, transparency and accountability. *(See S.8 of this Application).*
- Collaborating with like-minded others including concerned citizens and residents of the State who have had proven, damaging experience of the Irish Courts and who seek urgent reform of the institutions of State so as to align truthfully and credibly with the Rule of Law.

Almost without exception, each of these lawful efforts have met with coordinated unlawful resistance and obstructionism by the Irish establishment – and in particular (in the cases outlined in the full published Report) by the named accused parties—sometimes serially so—which in turn has provided incontestable evidence of repeat, systemic attempts to interfere with, obstruct, pervert and/or deny justice for the primary purposes of; (i) visiting unlawful and unwanted attentions on otherwise innocent parties, and/or (ii) shielding from exposure or accountability, persons in the employ of the State (or affiliates thereof) who are undeniably guilty of criminal acts.

We further note, explicitly, that in attempting to avail of our fundamental right to access justice, that we have now 'exhausted all domestic remedies' in seeking the rights due to us under the Rule of Law, and that the Irish State – chiefly in the form of the Department of Justice in context of its supervisory and oversight functions over the various arms of the Department – has completely and utterly failed in its constitutional duties to uphold the Rule of Law and protect our fundamental rights.

Indeed, that three Ministers of Justice in succession have either failed or refused to act on documented proofs of serious criminality by their agents and affiliates and/or have engaged in further criminal activity for the purposes of unlawfully suppressing and covering-up multiple proven, documented crimes – particularly regarding the obstruction of justice; the perversion of justice; and/or by interfering with the due and lawful administration of justice – which said offences have been committed variously by their colleagues, subordinates, and professional associates.

In context, we refer to the legislation quoted at Chapters 1 – 5 of the pilot I-I Report which not only requires residents and citizens of this State: (a) NOT to engage knowingly and directly in criminal activity; (b) NOT to facilitate or cover-up criminal activity; and (c) NOT to deliberately impede criminal investigations or prosecutions in the Courts; but (d) to actively report the same when knowledge of specific criminality comes to their attention, as quoted in the respective legislation; for example:

Criminal Justice Act 2011: S.19. [withholding information]—(1) A person shall be guilty of an offence if he or she has information which he or she knows or believes might be of material assistance in—(a) preventing the commission by any other person of a relevant offence, or (b) securing the apprehension, prosecution or conviction of any other person for a relevant offence, and fails without reasonable excuse to disclose that information as soon as it is practicable to do so to a member of the Garda Síochána.

S.17. [concealing facts disclosed by documents]—(1) Any person who—(a) knows or suspects that an investigation by the Garda Síochána into a relevant offence, other than an offence to which section 51 of the Criminal Justice (Theft and Fraud Offences) Act 2001 applies, is being or is likely to be carried out, and (b) falsifies, conceals, destroys or otherwise disposes of a document or record which he or she knows or suspects is or would be relevant to the investigation or causes or permits its falsification, concealment, destruction or disposal, shall be guilty of an offence.

(2) Where a person—(a) falsifies, conceals, destroys or otherwise disposes of a document, or (b) causes or permits its falsification, concealment, destruction or disposal, in such circumstances that it is reasonable to conclude that the person knew or suspected—(i) that an investigation by the Garda Síochána into a relevant offence.. ...applies, was being or was likely to be carried out, and (ii) that the document was or would be relevant to the investigation, he or she shall be taken for the purposes of this section to have so known or suspected, unless the court or the jury, as the case may be, is satisfied having regard to all the evidence that there is a reasonable doubt as to whether he or she so knew or suspected.

Criminal Damage Act 1991: *S.2. (3) A person who damages any property, whether belonging to himself or another, with intent to defraud shall be guilty of an offence.*

The fact that these, and many such similar offences

as listed in the I-I Report have been reported via official channels without any consequent sanctions, penalties or prosecutions of the named accused should be sufficient to raise alarm bells in the minds of any decent, right-thinking, law-abiding persons, and especially amongst those persons whose duty is to uphold the Rule of Law in this State.

We note in particular that a number of valid applications for criminal summonses under *S.10 of the Petty Sessions Act 1851* remain inexplicably (and unlawfully) 'on hold' in the Criminal Courts of Justice which said applications name several senior officials and office holders in proven criminal activity. That these are among many such valid applications which have met with coordinated, unlawful obstructionism by the very persons empowered and mandated to 'uphold the law and the constitution' and that despite these illicit activities being in overt, flagrant breach of Superior Court rulings and judgments that were issued as recently as 2016 that even the Superior Courts are now actively complicit in the suppression of these criminal applications and of the incontestable facts that ground them; leading to additional published accusations and charges as against those persons involved in unlawful, underhanded and disreputable 'business' in the Courts.

Criminal Law Act 1997: S.7.(2) Where a person has committed an arrestable offence, any other person who, knowing or believing him or her to be guilty of the offence or of some other arrestable offence, does without reasonable excuse any act with intent to impede his or her apprehension or prosecution shall be guilty of an offence.

Similar legislation is unequivocal as to what constitutes an offence under the law, including any additional acts of criminal concealment, obstructionism or denial of the facts which often includes collusive attempts to pervert justice via acts of perjury, fraud, conspiracy to deceive, to abuse due process and other unsanctioned contempts of Court, as well as serial obfuscations on the part of various 'Officers of the Court' for the purposes of exhausting the resources and resolve of otherwise credible complainants and litigants, which said offences are covered for example in *The Criminal Justice (Theft & Fraud Offences) Act, 2001* which, at S.6 explicitly states:

"(1) A person who dishonestly, with the intention of making a gain for himself or herself or another, or of causing loss to another, by any deception induces another to do or refrain from doing an act, is guilty of an offence."

Conclusion: On the basis of the evidence supplied and in the interests of expediency and clarity; it can accurately be summarised that the current, actual circumstances in Ireland are that a sizeable majority of senior officials and office holders – particularly in the justice-related arena – are actively involved in; (a) the commission of criminal acts; and/or (b) the concealment and cover-ups of those acts; and/or (c) in the unlawful 'targeting' by way of criminal harassment and focused persecution of persons who are perceived to be a threat to the unchallenged continuation of the said criminal activities.

> **"'Criminal organisation' means a structured group, however organised, composed of 3 or more persons acting in concert, that has as its main purpose or activity the commission or facilitation of one or more serious offences in order to obtain, directly or indirectly, a financial or other material benefit. 'Act' includes omission; and a reference to the commission or doing of an act includes a reference to the making of an omission."**
>
> *Abridged, from: The Criminal Justice Act 2006 & 2009 & the UN Convention against Transnational Organized Crime 2000.*

In short, that the evidence in the said I-I Report establishes beyond any reasonable doubt the existence of a *de facto* 'criminal organisation' (as per the respective statutory descriptions) operating undeclared within the auspices of the Irish justice system, wherein the individuals so involved are masquerading as 'officials and office holders'—civil servants, gardaí, lawyers, judges, TD's & Ministers—while illegitimately drawing down the benefits and supports due to those offices whilst simultaneously abusing the powers and authority available to them and violating the terms and responsibilities of those offices in knowing contravention of the Rule of Law, for the purposes of advancing collaborative, definitive, predetermined criminal ends.

Given the evidence provided, there can be no credible rebuttal to the claim that the Rule of Law is not – and has not – been applied in the conduct of the sample cases laid out in the pilot I-I Report, and, inasmuch as senior office holders with the statutory responsibility to address these critical failings have not only failed and refused to do so, but have repeatedly abused their positions to compound the crimes already committed, and have thereby rendered themselves subject to accusation and indictment; that the parallel allegation that a veritable 'criminal organisation' comprising so-called 'Officers of the Court' and their associates in the legal profession which subsists and indeed even thrives in the midst of our justice system under political patronage and statutory protection begs the inescapable question as to how much of this malfeasance needs to be occurring—for what amount of time and at what depth and persistence—and at how high the positions, before we unequivocally declare and accept the glaring reality; that other than in theory and being simply 'written on paper' that there is in effect no actual, genuine Rule of Law in Ireland?

This is an inescapable reality bound by serious questions that simply cannot be ignored if we are to maintain any national dignity or credibility on the world stage.

This point having been clearly made; let us now review other aspects of 'the problem' with a view to identifying credible and achievable solutions.

2. THE INHERENT LEGITIMACY OF OFFICES & INSTITUTIONS OF STATE

First of all we note the indisputable, self-evident fact that the tenure of any-and-all officials and office holders in this State is contingent upon their individual adherence to the Rule of Law and their respective positions as citizens of this State who are each, "subject to the law and the Constitution". Indeed, that the very existence of this State and its legal standing as a sovereign nation, as well as its continued membership of the European Union is predicated upon its adherence to the Rule of Law.

Of course, the various 'Offices of State' in-and-of-themselves are meaningless entities without an assigned, named 'Office Holder' who has the overall responsibility to direct, administer and supervise that Office's activities according to the law and the Constitution. Clearly, it is that person's moral and legal duty to ensure that the ethos, functions and culture of their respective offices truly complies with the law. Accordingly, any such prevailing 'responsibilities of office' rest entirely on the incumbent office holder, and the corresponding validity and authority of any such Office is in turn, wholly dependent upon that office holder's capacity, willingness and ability to carry out the functions of their Office according to the Rule of Law, and to direct their subordinates accordingly.

Conversely, should any assigned office holder prove incapable, unable or unwilling to carry out the functions of their Office, then naturally—as is provided for in *Article 35.4(i) of the Constitution* in the case of judges for example—those persons may be removed from Office on the grounds of 'incapacity'. And whilst it must be understood of course, that all such office holders are human, fallible and imperfect beings who may from time to time suffer lapses, errors or other failings of office that can reasonably be excepted to occur and therefore should, in most cases, be accepted and overlooked as the inevitable consequences of employing people rather than robots; that any such occasional 'errors or lapses' are vastly different in essence and in consequence, to the more sombre declaration that one is either 'unable or incapable' of carrying out one's statutory functions.

Similarly, any such office holder who engages in 'misconduct' or other inappropriate activities sufficient to jeopardise the authority of their Office, such as knowingly committing criminal offences in context of the same; renders their tenure of that Office immediately invalid, whereupon the said Office is consequently and ineluctably 'vacated' (in the legal-and-statutory sense) until such time as the invalid office holder is replaced.

It needs to be said of course, that if the misconduct goes unnoticed or unreported, that the offending office holder will invariably continue in position unperturbed, albeit as the now technically-illegitimate holder of an Office whose standing has been compromised and/or corrupted by the office holder's criminal activity. It also needs to be said – somewhat obviously – that if the said misconduct *is* in fact reported to the statutory authorities then there needs to be consequences according to law, otherwise there is in effect, no law at all.

And this is the predicament and conundrum that faces those of us who have chosen to live in a modern democratic State, an advanced 'first world' nation and a Member State of the UN, the CoE and the EU, where the Rule of Law is *supposed* to reign paramount.

*   *   *

"The Irish Times recently analysed the present Government's performance in relation to accountability to Dáil Éireann and came up with such a black picture that the Government Chief Whip, probably much to the dismay of his masters, accepted that it was *"deplorable"*. Senior ministers failed to appear in 75% of *"Topical Issue"* debates raised by back-bench TDs from all parties on each Dáil sitting day. 40% of such issues were dealt with by a Minister of State from an entirely different department who simply read into the record a pre-prepared script having had no personal knowledge of any kind in relation to the accountability issue being raised."

From; "THE CRISIS IN DEMOCRATIC ACCOUNTABILITY" *by Michael McDowell SC, Barrister and Columnist, former Attorney-General, Minister for Justice and Tanaiste.*

3. THE PROBITY, INTEGRITY AND LAWFUL FUNCTIONING OF DOMESTIC COURTS

With no intention of causing gratuitous offence or indeed of indulging in any exaggeration or overstatement, it needs to be said, quite objectively and dispassionately, that the circumstances we find ourselves in (as detailed in the I-I Report) are so far removed from any notion of 'the Rule of Law' or of genuine 'access to justice' — as to render the prospect of approaching the Irish Courts for a lawful remedy in any matters that threaten to expose the rampant misconduct, corruption and criminality ongoing 'in high places' to be utterly futile and pointless. The machinery of the law it seems, is not actually there to serve justice; but to service the often-illicit interests of connected elites. If one finds oneself by misfortune (or otherwise) in opposition to this cabal — well, prayer may well be one's only remaining option.

With due regard and respect to those individual judges who may indeed aspire to ethical conduct, those of us with intimate experience of the Superior Courts have come to the inescapable conclusion that there is so much overt and covert dishonesty, rule-breaking and blatant criminal contempt for the law going on in those elevated chambers as to render the Irish Courts as a national institution generally 'unfit for purpose' and indeed even legally redundant; and the respective named judges as being morally, ethically and professionally defunct — and therefore clearly and plainly 'unfit for office'.

The European Court of Justice (ECJ) established 6 criteria for the recognition of 'a competent domestic tribunal' to include the national Courts of Member States. *(See ECJ cases C54/96 & C-196/09)* These ask the following questions concerning the said Court(s):

1. Is it established by law?
2. Is it permanent?
3. Is its jurisdiction compulsory?
4. Does it have an *inter-partes* procedure?
5. Does it apply rules of law?
6. Is it independent?

Point No 1 requires that the Court, "is established by law". Unfortunately, no-one can produce the original *Commencement Order No 1* for the *1924 Courts of Justice Act,* which is *the* mother document that granted 'jurisdiction' (the lawful right and authority to operate) on all Irish Courts. This means, technically-and-literally, that there is NO evidence that our Courts were ever given legal standing (or vested jurisdiction) by the Government of the day. Notwithstanding the mindboggling scenario that this 'fact' presents us with, and the consequent bearing it has on *all* of the court cases heard between 1924 and 1961, and, since then, *all* of the cases that were initiated in the lower Courts; the plain fact of the matter is that if *Commencement Order No 1 of 1924* was never actually enacted (which does seem to be the case) then certainly, our Courts are not what they appear to be no matter what the optics are.

Yes, we have buildings that look like Courts, and we have lots of pretentious-looking people in wigs and gowns getting well-paid by the public to swan around with highfalutin airs and graces – and some of them even make legal pronouncements that are enforced by gardaí and bailiffs and prison officers.., but unfortunately, it may all be utterly invalid and void – all the way back to 1924!

Common sense would suggest that the question should be 'put to the people' – by referendum if needs be – as to what should be done? But instead, the legal establishment has recently decreed that the *1961 Courts (Supplemental Provisions) Act*, (which was actually grounded on the non-existent 1924 Act with nearly 40 direct references to it) has somehow since remedied the absence of any vested jurisdiction by simply carrying-over and amending legislation that was never even enacted in the first place!? Only the lawyers could have come up with that one! To be clear, the establishment is now trying to dismiss the inconvenient historical illegality of our Courts by simply ignoring the fact that the 1924 Act was never commenced, thereby putting an even bigger spotlight on an issue that raises questions about the overall legitimacy and legal standing of all Irish Courts today.

Raising this particular issue here may seem to be pettifogging in circumstances where we are arguing about the far more important principle of the very existence of the Rule of Law in Ireland – especially when our other points of contention are far more contemporarily (vs historically) relevant – but in circumstances where we are challenging the overall legitimacy of the Irish Courts as they stand and operate today, this technical-legal point simply had to be addressed and included.

For a better understanding as to how the law relates to 'Void' or non-existent Court Orders or other legal nullities, please see *"V: The Void Court Order"* on page 23 of the published I-I Report.

Point No 2 requires that the Court, "is permanent". But arguably (apart from those wonderful gothic buildings left to us by the British and the glitzy C.C.J. in Dublin) our Courts as legal institutions may not be 'permanent' *per-se* inasmuch as they appear NOT to have been granted jurisdiction in 1924 and thereby would have had NO domestic, statutory, legal validity to operate.

Point No 3 requires that the Court, "has compulsory jurisdiction". Unfortunately, like many legal terms, this one is somewhat indistinct and open to interpretation. 'Compulsory' for example can mean, "an essential component required to operate" or, it can imply that some sort of force (such as the threat of arrest, or fines, or seizure of property) may be deployed in order to compel compliance – right? 'Jurisdiction' on the other hand is defined as, "the extent of the power to make legal decisions and judgments". So, the phrase, "the Court has compulsory jurisdiction" could be understood as saying that; (i) jurisdiction *must be* bestowed upon the Court by the Government, and without it the Court *cannot* operate (which is a lawful fact); and/or (ii) that, under pain of penalty, the public is obliged to obey the rulings of the Court according to the limits of that Court's 'jurisdiction' (which is another lawful fact). 'Jurisdiction' in this latter context includes the Court's geographical location, the types of cases it can deal with, and/or the size of any penalty or damages award etc). But the immediate pressing question is, how can something that may not be lawfully in existence in the first place, have any sort of 'compulsory jurisdiction'? In addition, and setting aside the 1924 Act issue for a moment, adherence to the judicial oath of office is an *absolute* requirement for a judge's *vested* (personal) jurisdiction under *Article 34*. Accordingly if, as has been shown, our Courts are largely preoccupied with the covering up or facilitation of official crime, and in so doing, various 'Officers of the Court' including named judges are indulging in deliberate criminal activity..? Well obviously, this renders any purported 'jurisdiction' of that particular judge *and* of that Court—let alone any so-called *"compulsory* jurisdiction"— immediately invalid; that is, other than in the minds of a largely-unaware, confused and deceived public who live in fear of the consequences (police, fines, jail, losing loved ones into State care, etc..) of challenging this illegitimate cabal – or when refusing to comply with its unlawful diktats?

Point No 4 requires that the Court, "has an *inter-partes* procedure". This point is conceded inasmuch as our Courts are primarily structured to deal with cases on an adversarial basis between prosecuting and defending parties – which arguably, is not the most conducive environment to expedite justice. Many would argue for a more collaborative approach (especially in non-criminal cases) where joint resolutions could be agreed. On the other hand however, a confrontational setting does tend to increase costs and fees for the franchise. In any event, this 'inter-partes' requirement is supposed to be there to ensure that no one can win or lose a case without 'due process' and without a chance to have their say. What is not elucidated here is the fact that most legally-untrained persons who enter an Irish Court are immediately at an inter-partes disadvantage precisely *because* of the deliberately obscure and obtuse language being used, because of the confrontational setting, and because they are utterly bewildered by the tortuous, convoluted legal pantomime unfolding around them. Whatever 'inter-partes procedure' they may ostensibly 'participate in' by being present in Court is usually solely through their legal representative who may (and more often, may not) value a client's interests over their commission from the case. Other factors may gravely affect any supposed 'effective legal representation' of an all-but-dumb client. In short, it is our experience that simply having an 'inter-partes' procedure in place is no guarantee of genuine representation, nor of a fair hearing in an Irish Court, especially when so many other routine violations of truth, law and justice are being systematically ignored or disingenuously facilitated.

Point No 5 requires that the Court, "applies rules of law". Unfortunately, and based on our collective experience to date and upon all of the evidence in the I-I Report, it is clear that Irish judges do not apply 'rules of law' in any recognisably consistent or reliable basis. Some judges may, but most do not, simply because they don't have to. This is partly because of the stranglehold that 'The Benchers' hold over the legal profession and the career consequences for individual lawyers if-and-when they ever muster the courage to challenge judicial errors there-and-then in the Courtroom, especially when the more profitable alternative (for everyone in the franchise except the bewildered litigant) is to rack up endless appeal fees in the Superior Courts. Furthermore, when law is actually being applied (as opposed to when it is being completely and utterly ignored) it is usually being applied 'prejudicially and selectively' in favour of whichever party to the case has the requisite political influence or statutory locus, which blatant, thinly-veiled bias makes a complete nonsense of the concept and principle of, "applying the law – without fear or favour".

Point No 6 requires the Court to be, "independent". The inconvenient fact that Irish Judges are politically appointed in a most brazen fashion makes a complete nonsense of this requirement. Despite paltry efforts by the establishment to conceal these political sleights-of-hand through supposed 'robust independent recruitment and selection procedures' such as the admittedly "pointless and redundant" Judicial

Advisory Appointments Board (JAAB) which hasn't even held *one* formal interview in some 25 years of its existence, is statement enough. The added fact that even the tame national press opined; *"The JAAB camouflage is a laughable layer of obfuscation"* with its Board top-heavy with Judges, is sufficient to make the point that the JAAB is mere political tokenism wrapped up in smoke-and-mirrors designed to deceive and mislead the public. The plain, undeniable fact is that Irish judges are politically appointed, and remain embedded in the establishment. Accordingly, there is no genuine separation of powers. Period. *(See I-I Report p.72)*

To conclude this Section: It is our sincere position that the Irish Courts – as they currently stand – do not adequately fulfil these EU/ECJ criteria thus leaving Ireland without 'a competent domestic tribunal' or indeed without any properly-functioning justice system, which, if proven, would further endorse the requirement for an immediate *Part 2 Enquiry* and qualify the urgent establishment of *The Peoples Tribunal of Ireland*.

If we are to accept then, that the EU criteria for 'competent domestic tribunals' are not nearly being met, and that other troubling factors such as outlined here and in the I-I Report raise fundamental questions as to the overall statutory legitimacy of our Courts and of their general operational probity – then surely, someone in authority should be asking the all-too-obvious question as to how did we find ourselves in this sad and sorry mess in the first place, and what are we going to do about it?

Because, if these are not 'lawful courts' by express definition, then they are 'unlawful courts' (at best) and only 'courts' at all by mere virtue of the existence of the court buildings, infrastructure and staff. But these are courts without legal, moral or technical validity because they operate in direct violation of their constitutional terms of operation. For any such unlawful courts to continue to draw upon the resources of the State so as to force compliance with unlawful orders, judgments, instructions or directions under threat of penal consequences for the parties concerned, is of course yet another blatant violation of the constitutional requirement that our Courts (and judges by inseparable association) operate, *"subject to the law and the Constitution"* and, under the Rule of Law.

In conclusion, if we are to assess the overall merits, the probity, the integrity and the legitimacy of the Irish Courts against the 6-point checklist of the European Court of Justice, not to mention as against our own internal Court Rules and the *Article 34* requirement that the Courts be 'established according to law' then clearly, we are in a bit of a quagmire at best, and arguably in a serious legal and constitutional crisis that needs to be addressed as a matter of great urgency by the Irish State – and this even, before we take a closer look at the legalities that are contiguous to the Irish judiciary.

4. THE IRISH JUDICIARY: SELECTION, JURISDICTION, INCAPACITY & MISCONDUCT

The I-I Report establishes that a culture of selective contempt for – and abuse of – the law exists in the nation's Courts whereby certain judges in particular feel at liberty to engage in serious judicial misconduct for the purposes of protecting from accountability other agents of the State and/or of otherwise 'connected insiders' who are engaged in improper, corrupt or unlawful activities. Licence also appears to have been given to certain judges and various other 'Officers of the Court' to disrespect, mislead and deceive lay litigants in particular, and generally disregard their fundamental right to, *"a fair and impartial hearing before a competent, independent and impartial tribunal established by law"*. It hardly bears articulation what the fate is of those who are perceived to be 'politically inconvenient' or in any way a threat to the establishment. The role of the judge as a fair and impartial referee in a very lopsided game where the rules and the goalposts are being constantly (and illicitly) changed is practically unheard of, and anyone who is embedded within the State seems impervious to sanction or correction, no matter how grievous their offences against 'the Court' are.

These antagonistic intentions and dishonourable attitudes and behaviours fly directly in the face of the internationally-recognised and UN-endorsed *Bangalore Principles of Judicial Conduct* which should be at the forefront of any statutory considerations in the selection and appointment of persons to the Bench. Unfortunately, and somewhat ridiculously here in Ireland (and other than the general *pretence* of propriety which certain Irish judges are so adept at) it is the notable *absence* of those core values of, "independence, impartiality, integrity, propriety, equality, competence and diligence" that seems the best guarantee of being selected by one's political patrons or colleagues in the legal profession for a cosy appointment to the Bench. The fact that certain judges have appalling records in their previous careers as solicitors or barristers is telling enough. The added fact that they do NOT have to disclose their personal 'interests' (financial or otherwise) leaves open the suspicion and possibility (which has been proven a number of times) that any given judge could be subject to influence, pressure or profit such as to interfere with their supposed 'statutory independence'. But it is the accumulation of scores of serious complaints by ordinary members of the public that marks the overwhelming majority of Irish judges as having been politically appointed in the first place, with the clear, yet undeclared expectation – as is generally proven in their subsequent actions – that the protection of the status quo, however corrupt, trumps any naïve notions they might have of justice, impartiality or integrity. And whilst we must always make allowances for the exception to the rule, it is abundantly clear that 'the rule' here in

Ireland is that if you are NOT politically connected, and you are NOT willing to bat for the status quo, then you probably aren't going to find yourself on any Bencher's shortlist anytime soon. That is an appalling indictment of a profession that is supposed to comprise the very best of us; those who are genuinely wise, independent, impartial and fair; the guardians of law; and persons whose honesty and integrity can always and absolutely be relied upon.

Notwithstanding the unsettling backdrop of political insiderism in the judicial appointments process, statutory factors endow Irish Courts with the legal authority and jurisdiction to administer justice. These are laid out in the Constitution under Articles 34–38 and include (abridged):

- That Courts are set up according to law and operate within their respective jurisdictions. *[Article 34.1.]*

- That individual judges obey the law, respect the Constitution, and act within jurisdiction. *[Article 34.5(i)]*

- That judges abide strictly by their solemn Constitutional Oath of Office. *[Article 34.5(i)]*

- That judges respect the order of primacy of law, and comply with Superior Courts' Rulings.

- That judges are constitutionally 'capable' of carrying out their duties. *[Article 35.4(i)]*

- That judges do NOT engage in 'misbehaviour'. *[Article 35.4(i)]*

The constitutional requirement that judges are 'capable' of carrying out their duties requires an understanding of the physical, logistical, educational, and psychological demands of the role of judge. Accordingly, anyone who is technically 'incapable' of carrying out that role should not be appointed, or, if they demonstrate by their post-appointment behaviour that they are incapable, then according to the constitution, they may / shall / should be removed from office. Unfortunately, that is not happening.

Two pertinent issues immediately arise in our collective experience of the Irish Courts. Firstly, we need to acknowledge that a high proportion of those being appointed to the Bench are politically selected, and secondly, that a number of these appointees suffer from what is currently known as, 'antisocial personality disorder' or ASPD. This is a condition recognised by the *Diagnostic and Statistical Manual of Mental Disorders (DSM-5)* and is more commonly referred to as 'sociopathy' or 'psychopathy'. It is our position that persons so afflicted are entirely unsuitable for judicial office on the grounds that; (a) such a diagnosis renders them literally-and-psychologically 'incapable' of performing certain functions; and (b) that persons so afflicted are predicated towards certain typical behaviours – many of which result in actions that fall well beyond the bounds of mere 'misconduct'.

To clarify: In context of the lawful functioning of our Courts, it needs to be pointed out that the judges' oath of office (which is an absolute prerequisite for vested jurisdiction) has three identifiable aspects: (a) the literal-legal aspect that requires some academic awareness of how to correctly, "uphold the law – without fear or favour"; (b) an ethical-moral aspect that guides that proper application; and (c) a religious aspect that renders the oath-taker answerable to God.

Naturally, if the oath-taker is an atheist, then the oath is meaningless. Likewise, if the oath-taker intends to service his political patrons, friends and colleagues through his office at the expense of justice, then again, the oath is meaningless. Finally, if the oath-taker can be shown to be a clinical sociopath or psychopath, then that person is, literally-and-clinically "incapable" (in the constitutional, literal and personal-psychological sense) of accommodating any sworn oath that requires a *genuine* application of ethics, morality, or truth or justice – over one's own self-interests.

In short, whilst it may be understandable that the highest percentage of sociopaths and psychopaths in any given profession (second only to the CEO's of multinational corporations) are in the legal profession, and that any amount of solicitors or lawyers could therefore very well suffer from a disorder that makes lying, deception, theft, fraud, malicious perjuries, and the routine manipulation and exploitation of others just 'normal' behaviour for them; then equally, it needs to be said that the role of judge—as THE very person who must limit and curtail these sociopathic leanings in the Courts in the overall interests of justice—that *that* central role cannot possibly be assigned to yet another nefarious sociopath who may, or may not, actually perceive that any 'wrong' *per se* is being done by their counterparts even in the face of overt lawbreaking – which in any event the judge *should* be acting upon – and *should* be penalising.

The fact that our judges rarely sanction even serious transgressions by other agents of the State is one clear giveaway. But a more disturbing aspect of ASPD is the relative absence of conscience, morals or empathy which is often coupled with sadistic and/or predatory traits and behaviours, all of which when combined in any specific diagnosis of ASPD would most assuredly render the subject not only utterly unfit for high public office, but indeed for any position or role of 'service to the public' that requires honest, empathetic and insightful decision-making, and/or a willingness to protect others from the predatory and often-criminal attentions of one's colleagues in the legal profession.

And this, upon the logical, clinical and obvious premise that empathy is largely absent in the clinical sociopath, and that genuine 'service to others' is simply not in their nature. The *appearance* of service or of empathetic concern may be there, but there are no such intentions.

As to stated 'misbehaviour' being grounds for removal from judicial office, obvious examples would include for example; (i) the requirement that judges do NOT abuse their statutory powers or vested jurisdiction (where applicable). (ii) That they do NOT scandalise the Courts or bring the judiciary into disrepute by engaging in unethical, unprincipled, dishonest or disreputable behaviour whilst carrying out their judicial duties; and (iii) that they do NOT act in contempt of their own Courts by knowingly engaging in—or facilitating—overt-and-covert frauds, deceptions, forgeries, perjuries and other offences against justice.

Again, with respect to those judges not of our experience who may operate otherwise; it is the very existence and persistence of this sort of criminal misbehaviour by persons who are supposed to be beyond reproach that gives rise to an urgent need for some lawful alternative to these morally-compromised individuals and corrupted institutions which, in the blatant continuance of these illicit and unlawful activities, serves only to mock and abuse the public's faith and confidence in what has since devolved into a nefarious, autocratic farce; a charade dressed up to look like a justice system; a cabal of politically-connected insiders and subservient lackeys who have hijacked the institutions and organs of State for intrinsically dishonest, devious, selfish, malicious and/or criminal purposes.

Hence the truism that if a high proportion of senior judges are knowingly engaging in overt misconduct, misfeasance, malfeasance, deception, nonfeasance and other forms of dishonest and discreditable behaviour sufficient to ground valid allegations of *criminal* misbehaviour, then clearly, it cannot be said that those particular Courts and those particular judges are operating, "subject to the law and the Constitution", which is arguably, *the* preeminent constitutional qualifier of what does, and does not constitute 'a lawful Court' *[Article 34.1.]*. And this, in addition to the questions already raised about the historical legitimacy of the Irish Courts and their alignment with EU criteria.

Furthermore, inasmuch as any such criminal misbehaviour by sitting judges has been observed, documented and reported but nevertheless draws NO statutory responses or remedies from the executive, legislative or judicial branches of the State, then this, somewhat obviously, renders those branches of government—or at very least the individuals who head up each branch who have personal knowledge of these crimes—complicit after-the-fact in those documented offences, many of which come under the reporting obligations of the respective *Criminal Justice Acts*.

This leads us inexorably to the unsavoury question as to how many persons need to be involved in this criminal activity – and for how long and at what cost to the public, before we call a spade, a damned spade?

5. THE CASE FOR A 'PART 2 ENQUIRY' BY THE HOUSES OF THE OIREACHTAS

Notwithstanding the unambiguous terminology that renders all citizens and residents of this State "subject to the law and the constitution", it is now a recognised fact amongst many thousands of Court users, that the application of the law to any particular individual in Ireland is almost entirely contingent on one's local social standing; on one's position within the machinery of State; and/or on one's political connectedness; – rather than on any genuine concept of 'the Rule of Law'. Perhaps this is why all of the authorities approached to date have reverted to frantic 'ostriching' or 'stonewalling' – once they realised that the usual obfuscation, misdirection, intimidation, persecution and reprisals were just not working.

The 2020 I-I Report has proven beyond any reasonable doubt that the Irish Courts are giving preferential (and often prejudicially-unlawful) treatment to persons acting in an Official Capacity, and in doing so the Irish Courts are not meeting the requirements of Article 13 of the European Convention of Human Rights which requires, "*an effective remedy before a national authority notwithstanding that the violation has been committed by persons acting in an official capacity.*"

The Report also lists a number of senior 'Irish Officials and Office Holders' who consequently engaged in unlawful refusals of service; in misdirection, obfuscation, obstructionism and stonewalling and, as-and-when that approach failed, the cowardly DPP-driven reprisals resumed.

This is a morally-repugnant state of affairs and must be addressed by the incoming government as a matter of great and critical urgency. For to fail to do so is to fail those who have suffered so much already, and who have exhausted all other remedies in their desperate and wretched approaches to the State.

The *Houses of the Oireachtas (Inquiries, Privileges and Procedures) Act 2013* provides the Irish Government with the tools and authority to enquire into 'specified matters' including the conduct of Irish officials and office holders, and; *"a committee may conduct an inquiry into the removal or proposed removal of an officeholder (howsoever described) pursuant to a relevant provision."* Naturally, "a relevant provision" (howsoever described) would absolutely *have to* include the law of the land, given the requirement that all citizens and residents of the State are, "subject to the law and the Constitution". Indeed, the subsection following the above quote articulates some of those provisions and Office Holders that are explicitly referenced in the I-I Report. They include the power to remove from office the following office holder(s) for stated, "incapacity or misconduct":

The President (Pt 2,Ch.2 S.16) / Judges / the Comptroller and Auditor General / Officers of GSOC / Complaints Referee / the Ombudsman /

Chairman of Dáil Éireann / the Clerk of Dáil Éireann / the Clerk of Seanad Éireann / the Information Commissioner / the Languages Commissioner / Members of the Ombudsman Commission / Broadcasting Authority (etc)...

As to whether the conditions of, "incapacity or misconduct" have been met, the reader is respectfully referred back to the I-I Report, *"Criminality in the Irish Courts, and the absence of the Rule of Law",* where all of us, including senior office holders appointed by Government are subject to the Rule of Law (at least theoretically) and it is upon this fundamental position and upon the more specific arguments herein that we ground this formal proposal and indeed make lawful, respectful demand of the Irish Government that they initiate *Part 2 Chapter 1 Enquiries* under the said *2013 Act* into; (i) the legal status and efficacy of the nation's Courts; and (ii) into the behaviour and conduct of those officials and office holders named in pages 235-239 of the full I-I Report including the consequent detrimental effects on their respective Offices. Notwithstanding any 'official' requirement to redact those names in any formal Part 2 Enquiry, this action would require bringing *Article 35.4(i) Motions* as against any judges so named, and an *Article 12.10(i) Part 2, Chapter 2, S.16 Enquiry* into the unlawful and unconstitutional conduct—by omission or commission—of the incumbent President of Ireland.

The fact is, that we have an utterly untenable set of

circumstances, where not only is the legal-constitutional validity of certain institutions of the State under serious question; but the specific legal, moral and technical authority of the Courts is being grossly undermined and jeopardised by the actions of rogue and dishonest judges sufficient to render particular Courts at specific times absolutely and utterly 'unfit for purpose'.

When the Courts (and judges) so specified include several senior judges of the Superior Courts including the Supreme Court itself, then clearly we have a serious national problem – indeed a veritable constitutional crisis – which needs to be addressed with the utmost urgency if Ireland is to maintain any shambling pretence at democracy or adherence to the Rule of Law.

Likewise with several senior officials and office holders as named in the full I-I Report, who have all-but abandoned their responsibilities under the law, which clearly states that any unlawful 'act' – whether by commission *or omission* – renders the subject liable to criminal penalty under the law.

The Irish State now finds itself in a precarious position as to its ongoing sovereign status within the United Nations and as a Member-State of the European Union and of the Council of Europe, given the requirements that Member States; (i) respect the Rule of Law, and (ii) have a properly-functioning justice system; neither of which in actual effect— not in function nor in practice—are fixed operational realities in this State.

The Petitions Committee guidelines on the admissibility of a petition include whether it:

1. relates to matters on which the Houses of the Oireachtas have the power to act;

2. complies with Standing Orders and is in proper form;

3. is not sub-judice, i.e. does not relate to a case where court proceedings have been initiated and which is to be heard before a jury or is then being heard before a jury;

4. does not contain the name or names of individuals;

5. does not contain language which is offensive or defamatory;

6. is not the same as, or is not in substantially similar terms to, a petition brought by or on behalf of the same person, body corporate or unincorporated association during the lifetime of that Dáil/Seanad and which was closed by agreement of the Committee;

7. is not frivolous, vexatious or otherwise does not constitute an abuse of the petitions system;

8. does not require the Committee to consider an individual complaint which has been the subject of a decision by the Ombudsman, by another Ombudsman, or by a regulatory public body or a body established for the purpose of redress.

In respect of the disconcerting facts that: (i) the Joint Petitions Committee – along with the Justice & Equality Committee were officially 'disbanded' on January 14th 2020 upon the dissolution of the 32nd Dáil; and (ii) noting that we had served Part One of the I-I Report *"Criminality in the Irish Courts"* on the Government on January 13th this year; and (iii) that other than the Tánaiste advising us that he had forwarded the Report to the Minister for Justice, that there were NO other due responses; and (iv) that over 6 months later and upon attempting to resubmit a formal Petition that the Secretariat of the JPC advised us that, *"no submissions could be made.."* and that they *"had no information as to when the Committee might be reconvened or what the new rules might be"*. And (v) in light of the 20-or-so existing Petitions that are purportedly, *"Being Examined For Compliance With Standing Orders"* and which cannot of course move forwards without the existence of a Petitions Committee; we are left with the very unsettling realisation that not only has the State been 'functioning' through the Covid-19 crisis without any means of facilitating the public's concerns in alignment with this declaration..

"This parliamentary petitions system presents an important avenue for individuals to participate in the democratic process, through the petitions process. Members of the public are able to take their policy concerns directly to the heart of Parliament and to influence the parliamentary agenda."

Oireachtas Petitions website, July 2020

..but we are also being told that the petitions admissibility criteria could change at any time!? A more cynical person might observe that this would enable any future Joint Petitions Committee (if they so wished) to 'legitimately' move the goalposts in order to disqualify any otherwise-valid Petition wherein, for example, dozens of senior officials and office holders are accused of criminal activity.

It is regrettable to acknowledge that such a move would not only be typical in our experience of the reaction of the establishment, but it must of course be anticipated – given the frantic and desperate 'ostrichism' and stonewalling that has given rise to the creation of the I-I Report in the first place.

Accordingly, and in anticipation of whatever blocking, obstructing, delaying or obfuscating tactics that will no doubt be deployed against this Petition and Application for a Part 2 Enquiry, we qualify each of the 8 exiting guidelines on the admissibility of a petition as follows:

1. Yes, our Petition, *"relates to matters on which the Houses of the Oireachtas have the power to act."*

2. We cannot possibly know at this time if our Petition, "*complies with Standing Orders and is in proper form"* until such is clarified to us by the JPC Secretariat. (Which we are awaiting)..

3. No, the Petition, *"is not sub-judice, i.e. does not relate to a case where court proceedings have been initiated and which is to be heard before a jury or is then being heard before a jury"*.

4. No, the original 62-page I-I Report, *"does not contain the name or names of* (accused) *individuals"* other than; (i) where necessary to identify Court proceedings by title; (ii) in a segment of a High Court affidavit that provides necessary historical context; and (iii) by way of identifying the recipients of pertinent correspondence – all of which can be redacted, if required, before any formal resubmission of the amended Petition, noting the crucial fact that 'privilege' *per se* (being the main reason for anonymity) does NOT actually apply in circumstances where each individual so named has had multiple opportunities to challenge, rebut or denounce the allegations against them and/or issue legal proceedings for (alleged) defamation – which they have consistently failed or refused to do.

4a. For the avoidance of any doubt however, the Petitioner will make available to the Government without delay, a 50-page amended and redacted version of the same original 62-page I-I Report, to be known as *'The JPC I-I Report'*.

5. Other than language that accurately, explicitly and directly conveys the truth of the circumstances, the Petition, *"does not contain language which is offensive or defamatory"*.

6. No, this Petition, *"is not the same as, or is not in substantially similar terms to, a petition brought by or on behalf of the same person, body corporate or unincorporated association during the lifetime of that Dáil/Seanad and which was closed by agreement of the Committee."*

7. No, the Petition can not in any form be described as, *"..frivolous, vexatious or otherwise does not constitute an abuse of the petitions system."*

8. No, this Petition, *"does not require the Committee to consider an individual complaint which has been the subject of a decision by the Ombudsman, by another Ombudsman, or by a regulatory public body or a body established for the purpose of redress."* However, it should be clarified that the Petition DOES require the Committee to consider—amongst many affiliated criminal acts by Irish officials and office holders—an interconnected series of actions, decisions, and failures to act according to the Rule of Law, including a number of unlawful decisions by certain parties ostensibly with 'redress' responsibilities under the authority of the State. Most notable in this regard are the criminal allegations against named judges and senior office holders and the parallel applications for criminal summonses which were formally and validly applied for through the Courts but which have since (and variously) been unlawfully ignored / obstructed / denied / refused / and/or which remain suspended / on hold / shelved / inactivated etc., in direct and flagrant contravention of the law, of the Constitution and of Superior Court rulings and judgments as laid out in the said I-I Report.

In short, that this Petition refers to the wholesale, yet individual and particular failures and refusals of agents and agencies of the State to comply with their sworn, lawful mandate, under the Rule of Law.

6. THE CASE FOR THE ESTABLISHMENT OF THE PEOPLES TRIBUNAL OF IRELAND (PTI)

In seeking some sort of rational, credible and logical explanation for all of the routine contempt for the law and the Constitution ongoing in our Courts; for the repeat failures and refusals of any-and-all of the officials and office holders approached to date to respond in any meaningful way; and, whilst eliminating the implausible possibility that all of this routine malfeasance, misfeasance, obfuscation and stonewalling was merely the unfortunate result of truly astonishing levels of incompetence and stupidity and of ignorance of the law amongst some of the highest-placed legal professionals in the State; we have accordingly, arrived at the sorry but obvious conclusion that these illicit, unlawful and disingenuous activities are in fact, deliberate, conscious and knowing violations of the law which are being committed with scienter and malintent, in concert with others under the protection of their superiors, by various agents of the State and by 'Officers of the Court' including by named judges.

In other words, and as expounded upon in more detail in the I-I Report, our Courts and our judges are not only NOT doing their jobs properly – they are in many cases doing *exactly the opposite* inasmuch as they are perverting, interfering with and obstructing justice – and are doing so with the active knowledge and support of their colleagues and subordinates. In doing so they bring shame and disrepute to their noble professions, and personal disgrace upon themselves. They also render the legal validity, the statutory authority and the Constitutional jurisdiction of those Courts utterly null-and-void by their actions.

And meanwhile, where is *public* justice? No different to the rogue mechanic who damages cars instead of repairing them or who makes up invented problems so as to charge illicit workshop fees, any 'Officer of the Court' who defies or undermines genuine justice through dishonest means – and especially if he is doing so with a group of collaborators for devious, criminal ends. Well, what else should we call them other than a bunch of criminals!

This in turn begs the million-dollar question: what are we supposed to do when a proven criminal with high statutory standing and authority gives us orders that we know are illicit, unlawful, detrimental or just plain wrong!? As luck would have it, we do have an answer to that very question. Because it has already been endorsed by all respective authorities in the existing 'QTC Notices' that NO resident or citizen—and most especially, NO civil or public servant—is obliged to acknowledge or obey unlawful instructions, no matter who that person is (or indeed how scary they look). Consequently, there is no statutory, legal or moral obligation on any resident or citizen of this State to engage with the said persons. Indeed, it may be a criminal offence in its own right for any such subordinate person to comply.

Accordingly, this Declaration places all Irish authorities officially 'On Notice' of the unlawful status of a number of senior officials and office holders so complicit, and by association, their *de facto* abandonment of tenure of their respective Offices. Naturally, this creates a certain void in the statutory operations of the State – most notably in the justice-related arena, as we await an urgent remedial response in the form of a *Part 2 Enquiry* by the newly-appointed Government.

Based on our collective experiences at hundreds of court appearances and with scores of different judges (and with all due respect to those judges NOT of our experience who may in fact actually endeavour to respect their oaths of office) we hereby declare and assert our inalienable right under International, EU and domestic Irish Law to provide to the Irish public, 'a competent domestic tribunal' that will serve the interests of justice in Ireland to the limits of its power and authority in accordance with law; in alignment with *the Banqalore Principles of Judicial Conduct*; and according to the respective European Courts of Justice criteria; which said independent institution 'The Peoples' Tribunal' will be staffed by experienced, qualified experts in various fields for the purposes of establishing 'legal certainty' through the issuance of legally-binding rulings, findings and decisions. These mandates will be based precisely and literally on existing positive law, and will therefore have the *prima facie* force and authority of law, which in turn carries with it the vested jurisdiction that is inherent in law.

The legal basis for the establishment of this independent body rests primarily (albeit partially):

(i) On the various declarations of universal fundamental human rights which are binding on the Irish State but which are nevertheless being systematically flouted or ignored by agents and agencies of the State;

(ii) On the repeat failures and refusals of all of the statutory authorities approached to date to honour and respect those fundamental rights;

(iii) On the proofs of multiple criminal offences being committed by the said agents and agencies and the combined failure and refusal of the Irish authorities to apply the law;

(iv) On the existence of – and the continuous production of – various disingenuous, misleading and calculatedly-deceptive documentation issuing out of the nation's Courts which variously cannot and do not stand up to even the most cursory alignment with the truth, with the evidence and/or with existing law;

(v) The unexplained disappearance of, and the unlawful suppression and/or amendment of documents (for illicit and unlawful purposes) that were validly submitted to the Courts, or generated via the Courts;

(vi) The need for a competent, independent

authority to provide lawful, truthful and wherever possible, incontestable judgments and rulings based purely on the texts of existing positive law;

(vii) The need for authentic and tangible recognition of the person's fundamental right to access justice as guaranteed by *Article 6 of the ECHR* and in particular, *"the right that litigants should have an effective judicial remedy enabling them to assert their civil rights according to the Rule of Law"*. [*ECtHR: Beles & others v. the Czech Republic, 2002*]

The PTI as 'A Competent Domestic Tribunal'.

As noted in our critique of the Irish Courts, the European Court of Justice has established 6 criteria for the recognition of 'a competent domestic tribunal' which we quote again here as inherent qualifiers for the formal recognition of the PTI – especially in circumstances where it has been demonstrated that the Rule of Law is NOT being respected or applied with any measure of consistency by the institutions of the Irish State.

1. The PTI has been 'established by law': This rests on three pertinent facts and circumstances. First of all, *Article 40.6 of the Irish Constitution* allows for freedom of expression, opinion and association. Secondly, and concomitantly, the parties responsible for the setting up and establishment of the PTI do NOT require permissions or licences from the Irish State to do so notwithstanding the explicit provision in *Article 37.1.* for the setting up of 'other judicial bodies'. Thirdly, and perhaps most importantly, all Irish authorities and senior office holders were placed formally 'On Notice' of the proposed establishment of the PTI complete with the PTI Mission Statement and a copy of the I-I Report containing all of the reasoning and grounds for the same. Each was given an opportunity to raise any lawful objections they might have. They have not done so. Accordingly, and in specific context of the Irish establishment's longstanding application of the puerile tactics of persistent stonewalling and obfuscation – those cowardly twin intangibles – so frustrating to have to deal with and so blatantly contemptuous of those with legitimate and often life-changing concerns which can only be addressed by 'the authorities'.. that in light of their collective failures and refusals to respond as requested, that *The Peoples Tribunal of Ireland* has now acquired additional (albeit unnecessary) 'official' legal legitimacy and standing from the Irish State according to the specific terms of the PTI Mission Statement which was formally served upon them 'On Notice' and 'under seal' under the long-established and widely-recognised legal principle, *"qui tacet consentire videtur"* – silence implies consent. *(See S.8 following)*

2. The 'permanence' of The Peoples' Tribunal of Ireland is established; (i) by virtue of having a permanent address for the receipt of correspondence and for the holding of meetings and hearings, which functions may also be taken 'on circuit' to other locations or, conducted online as the situation and circumstances require. (ii) The PTI is also now 'permanent' inasmuch as it will continue operations in Ireland under the direction and governance of the PTI Council until such time as it can be demonstrated to all concerned that; (a) the Rule of Law has been properly and statutorily established in this State; (b) that there is no further need for the independent oversight functions provided by the PTI; and (c) that the PTI Council acknowledges the same.

However, in objective consideration of the current scale and depth of 'official wrongdoing' within the organs of the State, it is clear that if we are to maintain any semblance of sovereign legitimacy or national dignity that *some* organised body with the characteristics as outlined in the PTI Mission Statement *must* be urgently convened. It must further be realistically anticipated that inasmuch as the PTI will represent, 'truth, justice and transparency' on behalf of the Irish people, that the PTI may indeed become a valuable—if not indeed an indispensible asset and a partner—to any genuine attempts by struggling public bodies to understand, or properly adhere to the Rule of Law.

3. The 'compulsory jurisdiction' of the PTI rests primarily upon *Articles 37.1* and *40.6 of the Constitution*, and, somewhat ironically, upon the 'intrinsic vested jurisdiction' of the Rule of Law itself. Basic 'jurisdiction' (i.e. the permission and authority) to form and operate the PTI as a self-regulating body is ours by virtue of our inalienable right to free speech. The added jurisdiction to operate as 'a judicial entity' and/or as 'an association or union' is provided for in the Constitution.

Article 37.1. "Nothing in this Constitution shall operate to invalidate the exercise of limited functions and powers of a judicial nature, in matters other than criminal matters, by any person or body of persons duly authorised by law to exercise such functions and powers, notwithstanding that such person or such body of persons is not a judge or a court appointed or established as such under this Constitution."

Article 40.6.(i) & (iii): "The State guarantees liberty for the exercise of the following rights, subject to public order and morality: – (i) The right of the citizens to express freely their convictions and opinions. (iii) The right of the citizens to form associations and unions.

'Compulsory jurisdiction' in the form discussed earlier suggests that either; (i) the PTI must have formal authority bestowed upon it by an Act of the Oireachtas (for example); and/or (ii) that the public (or other entities of the State) are lawfully *obliged* to comply with the PTI's Rulings and Findings. Very interestingly, both of these interpretations are expressly qualified (somewhat ironically) first of all, by the State's 'QTC' refusal to object to the setting up of the PTI which failure granted us the 'official authority' to do so – if such were so required; and secondly, by the fact that the PTI will ONLY be making rulings or judgments strictly according to the written Rule of Law which is of course vested with its own 'intrinsic jurisdiction'. In other words, and failing the occasional error-in-law that might occur (and for which unlikely circumstance the PTI Rules allow for corrections and amendments) any formal Findings or Rulings that issue out of the Adjudicating Division of the PTI will always and in every instance only quote written 'positive' law sources in strict order of legal authority. In other words, inasmuch as the law itself has intrinsic jurisdiction that demands compulsory acceptance, acknowledgment and obedience, then so will any formal Rulings of the PTI demand lawful recognition; which said lawful recognition, in turn, establishes its 'compulsory jurisdiction'.

The seemingly-prohibitive reference in *Article 37.1* to 'a judge or court not dealing with criminal matters' refers solely to *the imposition* of criminal penalties such as imposing fines or imprisonment which are powers not being claimed by the PTI, because the *initiation* of criminal prosecutions in the nation's statutory Courts remains a general right under *S.10 of the Petty Sessions Act 1851* for all residents and citizens of the State.

An important distinction needs to be made between the concept of 'compulsory jurisdiction' and that of 'enforcement powers' by which a Court (for example) enforces its Orders by directing gardaí to take someone to jail or when a judge orders bailiffs to take someone's house. And this is where two of the most glaring anomalies of the Irish justice system repeatedly surface; (a) when an official or office holder deploys 'enforcement powers' when they have absolutely no jurisdiction to do so; and (b) when the same officials unlawfully *refuse* to employ their jurisdiction according to the Rule of Law. To put it more plainly, there couldn't be any *compulsory* enforcement of the law without the threat of jail or fines, and without some 13,000 gardaí ready to jump to a judge's command for example. Rogue judges are thus almost entirely dependent on the unquestioned obedience of gardaí, security, and Courts Service staff to enforce directions from the Bench – even when there may be no legal validity to those directions.

This is why *Article 37.1.* makes a distinction between civil and criminal matters, and why the only course of action for the PTI in the case of needing to 'enforce' its Rulings will be to return to the establishment by way of approaching the Garda Síochána, the Courts or the Government with Rulings and Findings that will oblige them under the law, to act according to the Rule of Law. The open publication of the same Rulings and Findings – especially if picked up by the mainstream media – may also serve to encourage and promote the appropriate, lawful responses by the statutory authorities, including by the enforcement arms of the State; An Garda Síochána, the DPP's Office and the Criminal Courts (no pun intended). This is NOT to say however, that any and all individuals who are members of the PTI do not still have full residual jurisdiction and authority to; (i) deploy existing powers of citizen's arrest either singularly or as a collective, and/or; (ii) lodge 'common informer' applications in their own names for criminal summonses under *the Petty Sessions Act* as per paragraph '(v)' in the PTI Mission Statement.

4. The PTI will have *fair and equitable* 'inter partes' procedures according to the Rule of Law.

5. The PTI will apply rules of law in strict accordance with written 'positive' law. In particular, the PTI will NOT indulge in unnecessary convoluted legalese; it will NOT entertain unsubstantiated hearsay or any materials in evidence that are not factual and self-evident; and will NOT generate 'opinions' *per se* other than qualified and necessary, explanatory commentary by the adjudicators (on the PTI website) on any apparent conflicts between aspects of law that do not have a clear order of supremacy.

6. Independence. Notwithstanding the liberty of any and all individuals, agencies or institutions whether private, commercial and/or statutory, to avail of the resources and published Rulings of *The Peoples Tribunal* according to standard PTI procedures; the PTI will remain completely independent of the State, of politics and of vested interests. In short, and inasmuch as it is capable of doing so, the PTI intends to provide to the Irish people a model of legal integrity and judicial propriety such as to set the standard for our beleaguered justice system.

Closing: For the avoidance of any doubt or confusion, and in the event we may have inadvertently misinterpreted or misunderstood the respective legislation, or otherwise breached or overlooked some pertinent issue or law; and, in the overall interests of transparency and accountability, we hereby invite the various officials and office holders who may be named in the full I-I Report, *"Criminality in the Irish Courts and the Absence of the Rule of Law"* or who are otherwise affected by the existence and proposed actions of *The Peoples Tribunal of Ireland* to respond to this Declaration with any observations, commentaries, suggestions or objections you may have to the continuation of *The People's Tribunal* as outlined herein and as referenced in the said I-I Report, noting (respectfully) that we cannot and will not accept any generic or unsigned responses which do NOT address the crucial underlying question as to where the public are supposed to go for redress or remedy when there is so much evidence of unchallenged criminal wrongdoing; of contempt for the Rule of Law; of dishonesty, collusion, perjury and fraud in the Courts; as well as specific unlawful violations (by commission or omission) of their constitutional oaths or terms of office by the preeminent authority figures in this State, particularly in the period March 2011 to January 2020 and most notably by the incumbents of the following offices and institutions:

- The Office of the President of Ireland.
- The Office of the Taoiseach.

- Specific Council of State Members including the Attorney General.
- The Irish Government – and particularly the last three Ministers for Justice.
- The Association of Judges of Ireland – and several named members of the judiciary including the Presidents of all five Courts in the period February 2012 – July 2019.
- The Bar Council – and several named Barristers.
- The Office of the DPP, including the Director, the Chief Prosecuting Solicitor and other senior staff members as named in the I-I Report.
- Certain persons in the employ of the Chief State Solicitor's Office (CSSO).
- The Law Society of Ireland – and numerous named members of the solicitors' profession.
- The Irish Human Rights Commission, and the Chairwoman in particular.
- The Office of the Ombudsman.
- The Child and Family Agency (TUSLA) and the respective Ministers in charge.
- The Courts Service – and numerous named employees including current and previous CEO's.
- An Garda Síochána – and several named members of various ranks including Commissioners.
- The Garda Síochána Ombudsman Commission (GSOC).

In conclusion: it is sincerely hoped and expected that the labours of *The Peoples Tribunal*—albeit being an independent non-statutory body—will be welcomed by the Irish Establishment and by legal professionals and by honest and conscientious members of the judiciary in particular, given the documented dearth of intelligible outcomes to so many issues, disputes and cases being brought before the Irish Courts. It is hoped that the arrival of a genuinely independent body that is publically committed to truth, honesty and integrity; to genuine service of the people; and to providing legal clarity and certainty for those institutions of the State who are clearly struggling with the concept; that this will surely receive a warm and enthusiastic welcome on the national stage.

Despite the said 'limited powers of compulsory enforcement', *The Peoples' Tribunal of Ireland* can and will serve the Irish State and its people during any period of necessary reorganisational reform by providing for those essential justice-related services that are due to the people which are essential to good governance, and which said crucial services—currently effectively absent in any consistent or reliable form in this State—are incumbent on the Irish Government to provide to the people, under the Rule of Law.

That in the continued absence, failures and/or refusals of the Irish Government to provide those services and guarantees under the Rule of Law, then it rests upon the residents and citizens of this

State to lawfully provide for the same, or, to fail in their moral and patriotic duty.

We believe that the incoming Irish Government must now act with all due diligence in addressing what we have shown and demonstrated to be, 'a crisis of criminality in our Courts' and that the particular circumstances as outlined in the full published I-I Report, *"Criminality in the Irish Courts and the absence of the Rule of Law"* [ISBN: 978-1-906628-88-8] clearly warrant an immediate and unqualified *Part 2 Enquiry* by *Dáil Éireann* under the terms of *the Houses of the Oireachtas (Inquiries, Privileges and Procedures) Act 2013,* subject to whatever redactions or amendments are required under the Act in specific reference to the 50-page 'JPC Version' of the original 62-page pilot I-I Report that was served on the Irish authorities on January 13th 2020, and which 50-page JPC (redacted) version accompanies this Application.

We hereby swear to the truth and the contents of this Declaration and appeal to the Irish Government in the form of the respective Committee(s), TD's, and/or Ministers of State to enquire without delay into the matters raised herein with a view to taking the appropriate action under the Rule of Law.

Thank you for your time and consideration.

Signed / Authorised etc.

PTI Executive, July 2020
On behalf of the PTI Council

7. THE SOLICITORS, BARRISTERS AND JUDGES NATIONAL FRANCHISE

"Judges must have at least 10 years' experience as a barrister or solicitor before being appointed to the District Court and at least 12 years' experience before being appointed to the High Court, the Court of Appeal or the Supreme Court."

Citizen's Information.ie, July 2020

By law, and according to the judge's constitutional oath, judges must be independent and impartial. But the reality on the ground is that control of the Irish Courts has been consigned to a collection of lawyers and judges who effectively operate as a national *franchise*, i.e. *"An authorization granted by a government (or company) to an individual or group enabling them to carry out specified commercial activities."*

Franchises operate under business rules for commercial gain. Courts are supposed to be in the business of justice. Yet the Courts Service, a commercial operation listed on the Companies Register states that it is, *"funded by the Irish State"* yet holds Court Funds of 2 Billion which are managed by an Investment Committee that is chaired by the President of the High Court.

The Courts Service Board likewise, carries a majority of judges who are responsible for the overall management of the Courts despite their purported 'statutory independence'. These are the people who make up the Court Rules that will apply when they switch from their franchise-related duties to the business of delivering justice. And, make no mistake, a business—and a very profitable one at that—it most certainly is; at least, for those inside the franchise.

This Benchers / Bar Association / Law Society / Courts Service & Department of Justice franchise thus controls all aspects of the delivery of justice in Ireland – and all of the members of the franchise know their place and role. Solicitors and Barristers who come before the Court are obliged to defer to judges – and judges expect the same. The question arises however, is this a business franchise, or, are we genuinely in the business of delivering justice?

Most litigants, completely unaware of this unacknowledged franchise, come before the Courts with naive notions of justice, not realising that they are greatly disadvantaged from the start and, despite their lawful entitlement to, *"an effective remedy before a fair and impartial tribunal"* that their chances of this rely almost entirely upon the proper application of EU Law, which frankly, is rarely in the interests of the Irish franchisees.

Unfortunately for the franchisees; Irish citizens voted in the Lisbon Treaty to make the Irish Courts and the Bar Association subject to and dependent upon European Law. But certain parts of EU Law that apply to human rights in particular are inconvenient to the Irish franchise, which is why we see Irish judges so often subverting or ignoring EU Law. This of course, is technically 'unlawful'.

Somewhat ironically, the combination of the supremacy of EU Law and the unlawful resistance of the Irish Courts franchise to defer to the same, provides not only the opportunity, but the necessity for the establishment of a national Court which acknowledges and applies EU Law.

Furthermore, and in light of the open defiance of the State to matters and policies that have been deemed 'unlawful' by the EU including VRT (excise duty); the (no jury) Special Criminal Courts; the protection of tax loopholes for multinational corporations; Ireland's carbon emissions failures; and the political appointment of judges for example, there is also the deliberate misinterpretation of important EU Directives so as to *protect* corporate operations and vested interests including the misuse of GDPR to *enforce* secrecy; the contrived application of anti-discrimination laws; and the neutralisation of anti-corruption legislation that might otherwise see Irish office holders being held to account.

Article 6.1 of the Constitution is unambiguous. *"All powers of government, legislative, executive and judicial, derive, under God, from the people, whose right it is ..to decide all questions of national policy.."* The Irish People voted for membership of the European Union and for the fundamental rights expressed in the *European Convention of Human Rights,* and the transposition of the same into Irish domestic law in 2003.

The PTI will provide the Irish public with 'legal

certainty' according to EU and ECHR Law, whilst simultaneously highlighting the demise of an outdated franchise, political in essence, which urgently needs to align itself with the democratic wishes of the people, and update its operations and mechanisms to properly reflect the progress being made in the global quest for genuine, collective, social justice.

The PTI will be a direct asset to the Irish State in specific context of EU Law inasmuch as it will comprise qualified professionals in various fields who are each experts in their own right. The PTI will produce short, succinct and clear Rulings in accordance with EU Law under the guidance of these experts including by internationally-trained lawyers working as volunteers in the public interest.

The invitation remains open to any professionals in any field – or indeed to any persons with knowledge or experience that will help the Tribunal in its work, to contact the PTI to see where they might help to ensure that Ireland maintains its place as a modern democratic republic with a properly-functioning justice system that genuinely respects the human rights of its own people.

*   *   *

8. FURTHER LAWFUL AUTHORITIES FOR THE ESTABLSIHMENT OF THE PTI

As explained in the respective texts and publications served on the Irish authorities as referenced in this book, the core legal authority for PTI operations is the Rule of Law itself. Specifically, that the 'intrinsic vested jurisdiction' of the Rule of Law provides the PTI (and indeed any other party) the lawful right and authority to produce literal and precise *interpretations* of the application of the Rule of Law, especially in circumstances where the Irish State is repeatedly failing the people in this regard.

'The Rule of Law' is not to be confused with the similar-sounding phrases, "*a* rule of law" or mere "rule *by* law" (as further clarified in the I-I Report) but refers explicitly to *the Rule of Law* (in capitals) which is a universally-recognised set of principles that encompasses fundamental human rights.

In particular, the PTI will *only* deal with submissions in context of what is known in legal circles as 'positive law'. 'Positive' in this context does not mean 'positive vs negative' *per se*, but refers to the fact that these laws have been 'posited' (or deposited) in writing, meaning literally 'on the record' in written form, which arguably should leave little room for errors or misinterpretation. When coupled with an understanding of the various different *types* of laws and in which order of precedence they should be applied, along with an appreciation of how the jurisdiction of various courts, individual judges or other agencies determine the reach, the limitations and/or the power-and-authority of each particular entity to interpret, apply and/or enforce the law; one arrives at a relatively simple formula under which the Rule of Law can be documented. It is the position of the founders of PTI—and one of the key grounds for the establishment of the PTI in the first place—that many of the serial errors, mistakes, violations and misapplications of the law which emanate out of the Irish Courts could be rectified—at least on paper—by the proper interpretation of the law.

This 'proper interpretation of the law' will be the central pillar upon which PTI operations will be based, and, in making those considered literal interpretations, we will be scrupulous in avoiding convoluted legalese and formal Latin, and will not indulge in any unnecessarily elaborate and tortuous 'legal opinions' which in many cases offer little clarity on the law and seem designed (whether intentionally or otherwise) to complicate and obfuscate matters instead of simply applying the Rule of Law in its most elementary and authoritative form, based *solely and explicitly on written positive law*.

To be clear, this PTI endeavour is NOT 'practicing law' *per se*. This is *interpreting* the law. The 'QTC Notices' following outline the general terms under which the PTI claims its lawful authority to do so.

THe following 'QTC' Notices were served on the authorities between 2016 and 2020 without any due or proper responses. 'QTC' 4 makes clear reference to other pertinent texts including this *Indictment & Application to Impeach* and to the published book: *"Criminality in the Irish Courts and the absence of the Rule of Law"* which contains a detailed listing of many EU and domestic laws, the persistent violations of which have created the legal, moral, constitutional and jurisdictional void that will now be filled by *The Peoples Tribunal* so as not to jeopardise Ireland's continued membership of the UN, the CoE and the EU. For the sake of clarity however, other primary legal principles upon which the authority of the PTI is established; to interpret positive law and issue formal Findings & Rulings includes:

- The right of access to justice
- The right to fair procedures
- The right to a fair trial
- The right to a fair hearing
- The right to equality of arms
- The right to access a lawyer
- The right to adversarial proceedings
- The right to a reasoned decision
- The right to be informed of proceedings
- The right to the independence and impartiality of 'tribunals' (courts)
- The right to legal aid in criminal proceedings
- The right to be advised, defended and *effectively* represented in criminal proceedings
- The right to accuracy of the record
- The right *not* to be subjected to 'excessive formalism'

- The right to adequate time and facilities to prepare
- The right of access to the case file
- The right to legal aid in appeal hearings
- The right to an effective remedy
- The right to a presumption of innocence
- The right of the court to overrule or overturn a decision by the DPP to prosecute
- The right to a genuine, authentic appeal system
- The right to be compensated upon proof of criminal wrongdoing by the State

..and upon these aspects of positive, written law.

- *THE UNIVERSAL DECLARATION OF HUMAN RIGHTS (UDHR) – 1948*
- *THE EUROPEAN CONVENTION ON HUMAN RIGHTS (ECHR) i.e. The Convention for the Protection of Human Rights and Fundamental Freedoms - 1953*
- *THE INTERNATIONAL COVENANT ON CIVIL AND POLITICAL RIGHTS (ICCPR) - 1966*
- *THE UNITED NATIONS BASIC PRINCIPLES ON THE INDEPENDENCE OF THE JUDICIARY - 1985*
- *THE COUNCIL OF EUROPE'S EUROPEAN CHARTER ON THE STATUTE FOR JUDGES - 1998*
- *THE (UN DRAFTED) BANGALORE PRINCIPLES OF JUDICIAL CONDUCT (OHCHR) – 2003*
- *THE EUROPEAN CONVENTION ON HUMAN RIGHTS ACT 2003 (ECHR ACT)*

And finally, the simple fact that on the evidence produced and other than sporadically, in random Courts and by occasional judges, that there is in fact NO legitimate, consistent 'competent domestic tribunal' that operates specifically and expressly under the Rule of Law in this State other than *The Peoples Tribunal of Ireland*.

'QTC 1' – NOTICE & CONSTITUTIONAL DECLARATION – August 2016

This formal NOTICE is hereby presented and served in regards to our fundamental human rights & in support of the constitutional position; that we are indeed guaranteed by inalienable right the confirmed protections of the Irish Constitution and those of the European Union and cannot lawfully be instructed, coerced or directed by any agents of the Irish State to act in contravention of these fundamental doctrines, nor to knowingly engage in unlawful, unconstitutional or criminal activity, and the State is hereby held strictly liable for any such breaches, including for any physical or psychological injuries or distress caused, and for all related costs and expenses.

1. Irish judges ARE subject to the law and the Constitution.

2. Members of the public ARE entitled to a fair hearing in the Irish Courts.

3. Judges of the District Court, Circuit Court and High Court ARE obliged to adhere to Supreme Court rulings, decisions and directions.

4. When any person in the pay of the State commits a criminal offence, they ARE subject to justice in our Courts in the same way as the tax-paying public are.

5. If any given judge deliberately breaks the law, the Constitution, their solemn Oath of Office or any other Act or Statute in the Courtroom; then any such hearing, or any decisions or pronouncements so rendered are, self-evidently, void and invalid.

6. Members of the public are NOT obliged to comply with unlawful, unconstitutional or criminal directions from any statutory authority figure such as a member of An Garda Síochána, by Courts Service staff or by members of the

Judiciary.

7. Law-abiding members of the public ARE guaranteed their constitutional safety and will NOT be unlawfully assaulted, injured or incarcerated whilst in the Courtroom.

8. All citizens and residents of this State have the right to issue private criminal proceedings, without cost or hindrance, against ANY other person, citizen or employee of the State under the terms of *The Petty Sessions (Ireland) Act 1851*.

9. Any such application, provided there is *prima facie* evidence of the crime alleged (and failing any extraordinary circumstances) MUST be dealt with on the day.

10. Notwithstanding the above, statutory provisions DO exist for the investigation of—and the removal of—judges of the various Courts for stated, *'incapacity, infirmity, misbehaviour and/or misconduct'* (in general or on specific occasion):

- S. 73 of The Courts of Justice Act 1924
- S. 21 of The Courts of Justice (District Court) Act 1946
- S. 10.1 (iv) of The Courts (Supplemental Provisions) Act, 1961
- S. 9 of The Houses of the Oireachtas (Privileges and Procedures) Act 2013
- Article 35.4 (i) of the Irish Constitution

ENDORSED *'QUI TACET CONSENTIT'* AUGUST 2016
By: **The President of Ireland**, *Michael D. Higgins;* **An Taoiseach** *Enda Kenny TD;* **Minister for Justice & Tánaiste** *Frances Fitzgerald TD;* **Garda Commissioner** *Nóirín O'Sullivan;* **Attorney General** *Marie Whelan;* **Director of Public Prosecutions** *Claire Loftus;* **Chief Justice** *Susan Denham (and any and all State-sponsored affiliates or subordinates thereof).*

'QTC 2' – NOTICE & DECLARATION – May 2019

1. ALL residents and citizens of this State – without exception – are subject to the law and the Constitution.

2. In addition, 'Irish officials' including civil servants, public servants and office holders are bound by their respective Codes of Conduct / Oaths of Office / Customer Charters.

3. Any non-statutory; (i) denials; (ii) inordinate delays; (iii) unqualified refusals; (iv) unexplained failures or departures from; and/or any (v) deliberate, calculated, reckless, negligent or conscious abuses of service due to members of the public, or to other agents or agencies of the State, would constitute a *prima facie* violation of the respective regulations.

4. Where any such violations can be attributed to; (a) dishonest, disingenuous, fraudulent, collusive or malicious actions or intentions on the part of the offender(s) and/or; (b) to discriminatory, prejudicial, unjust or inequitable motives; for the purposes of (c) visiting punitive, detrimental, unlawful or unconstitutional consequences, and/or amercement and personal distress on the persons suffering the said violations; that said violations would constitute *"corrupt"* and/or *"criminal"* acts as defined in the respective *Criminal Justice Acts:*

(i) "corruptly" includes acting with an improper purpose personally or by influencing another person whether – (a) by means of making a false or misleading statement; (b) by means of withholding, concealing, altering or destroying a document or other information, or; (c) by other means.

(ii) a crime or offence (or criminal offence) is an act

harmful not only to some individual but also to a community, society or the state ("a public wrong").

5. When any such violations are committed in context of; (i) the offender's potential advancement in their statutory/ official role; (ii) for their own or another's personal benefit; and/or (iii) in *de facto* expectation of the same; that such would constitute a *"consideration"* or *"advantage"* as defined in *the Criminal Justice (Corruption Offences) Act 2018, & EU law.*

6. When and where any such violations are knowingly committed in context of legal proceedings, that such would also constitute 'offences against the administration of justice'.

7. That any knowing compliance, assistance or facilitation of any such improper or unlawful acts by any other person would constitute direct complicity with any such unlawful acts.

8. That as per the respective Irish and EU legislation, it remains unlawful for any resident or citizen of this State to knowingly participate in unlawful, corrupt or criminal activities.

As endorsed April-May 2019 by the Offices of: (i) The President of Ireland; (ii) The Taoiseach; (iii) The Chief Justice; (iv) The Attorney General; (v) The Minister for Justice; (vi) The DPP; (vii) The CSSO.

IRISH CONSTITUTION, ARTICLE 40.1.

"All citizens shall, as human persons, be held equal before the law."

STATEMENT & DECLARATION
('QTC 3' – March 2020)

This document acquired force of law *'qui tacet consentit videtur' (silence implies consent)* March 9th 2020

1. Natural law (or moral law) is unwritten law that defines what is fundamentally 'right and wrong'.

2. Positive law is written law which defines what is 'legal or illegal' at any given time, in any place.

3. Four primary sources of *positive* (vs. natural) law apply in Ireland. In order of supremacy these are: (i) European Union Law. (ii) The Irish Constitution. (iii) Irish Legislation. (iv) Common Law & Case Law.

4. Secondary sources of positive law are known as 'statutory instruments' including; (a) ministerial orders, (b) governmental regulations, (c) operational rules, and (d) bye-laws (for example). These are delegated to regulatory bodies and local authorities. But they **must** be consistent with, and based on, the legislation adopted by the Oireachtas; otherwise they can be challenged in the Courts.

5. To contravene the law by any act or omission is to commit an unlawful, illicit and/or criminal act. "Lawbreaking" is also variously defined as; *'crime, breach, malefaction, misbehaviour, misconduct, misdeed, misfeasance, malfeasance, nonfeasance, transgression, trespass, violation & wrongdoing.'*

6. Accordingly, any person who, with full knowledge, awareness and understanding of the same, deliberately and knowingly: (i) disregards, (ii) ignores, (iii) defies; (iv) disobeys; (v) contravenes, (vi) breaches, (vii) flouts, or (viii) violates any such primary or secondary source of

law is—by virtue of the said illicit act or omission—committing a *prima facie* offence against the said law and is subject to the criminal penalties and/or legal consequences, if any, that apply in those circumstances.

7. Any such offending person including any Irish officials or office holders who engage in lawbreaking either; (a) in their private capacity as residents or citizens; and/or (b) in context of their public role or position, are subject to the respective legal consequences by way of: (i) criminal complaints to An Garda Siochána, and/or (ii) prosecution by the DPP; and/or (iii) by way of private, criminal prosecution under *S.10 of the Petty Sessions (Ireland) Act 1851*, and/or (iv) are also subject to legitimate citizen's arrest as per the terms of *S.4 of the Criminal Law Act 1997* & *S.12 of the Criminal Damage Act 1991*.

8. In particular, any Irish judge who, with full knowledge, awareness and understanding of the same, deliberately and knowingly: (i) disregards, (ii) ignores, (iii) defies; (iv) disobeys; (v) contravenes, (vi) breaches, (vii) flouts, or (viii) violates any such *primary* source of law whilst engaged in their role as judge is—by virtue of the said illicit act or omission—in added violation of: (a) *the Universal Declaration of Human Rights*; (b) *The International Covenant on Civil and Political Rights*; (c) *The United Nations Basic Principles on the Independence of the Judiciary*; (d) *The Council of Europe's European Charter on the Statute for Judges*; (e) *The European Convention on Human Rights* (ECHR); and (f) *The (UN Drafted) Bangalore Principles of Judicial Conduct*—and any such offending judge is therefore committing a *prima facie* criminal offence as against the administration of justice, which in turn would constitute literal 'judicial misbehaviour' as per the terms of *Article 35.4(i) of the Irish Constitution*, which said 'misbehaviour' is grounds

for impeachment and removal from office.

9. "Incapacity" is the second criteria under which a judge may be removed from office. Accordingly, should it be demonstrated that any given judge is physically, mentally or psychologically 'incapable' – or indeed has been rendered incapable of lawfully conducting his office through personal, moral, ethical, political or financial compromises, that any such judge should be removed from office.

10. Where proofs or supported allegations of judicial misbehaviour or incapacity are formally made known to any Member of Dáil Éireann or Seanad Éireann, the Constitution requires that the said person(s) refer the matter to the Government as per the terms of *Article 35.4(i) of the Constitution.*

IRISH CONSTITUTION, ARTICLE 40.3.

"1° The State guarantees in its laws to respect, and, as far as practicable, by its laws to defend and vindicate the personal rights of the citizen.

2° The State shall, in particular, by its laws protect as best it may from unjust attack and, in the case of injustice done, vindicate the life, person, good name, and property rights of every citizen."

The European Court of Justice uses 6 criteria to qualify 'a competent domestic tribunal'. These are fully discussed beginning on p.21 of this Booklet.

QTC 4' NOTICE & DECLARATION

*This formal Notice & Declaration is hereby served on all Irish authorities July 1st 2020

1. As an elected Official and/or Office Holder of this State I acknowledge that the sovereignty of the Irish State and its continued membership of the United Nations, the European Union and the Council of Europe is predicated on the genuine statutory adherence of the institutions of the Irish State with the Rule of Law.

2. I further acknowledge the statutory obligation on all Irish officials and office holders to carry out their official functions and duties in full accordance with the law and the Constitution.

3. I acknowledge receipt of the condensed version of the 2020 Report by the *Integrity Ireland Association* entitled, *"Criminality in the Irish Courts – and the absence of the Rule of Law"* and of the self-evident contents therein.

4. Inasmuch as the said Report documents the activities of listed officials and office holders; I recognise that the sum contents of the said Report indicates serious, repeat, critical failures by the said named persons to comply with their statutory obligations to respect the Rule of Law.

5. I acknowledge in particular the evidence of repeat, systemic, criminal activities by some named accused, many of whom hold high office in Government and in the Courts, and of the parallel failures of the justice system to hold the said persons accountable according to Law.

6. I acknowledge the ineluctable truism; that of the consequent, collective and cumulative, systemic-and-

endemic failures of the respective associated offices and institutions, to adhere to the Rule of Law.

7. I concur that Ireland *must* have an authentic, functioning justice system complete with valid domestic Courts established under law as per *Articles 34-38 of the Constitution,* and as per the 6-point criteria established by the ECJ.

8. That inasmuch as individual officials and/or office holders are clearly engaged in dishonest, unethical, amoral, unjust or unlawful activities, that such would render their tenure unconstitutional and invalid and would comprise grounds for referral to the *Houses of the Oireachtas* either for impeachment under *Article 35.4 of the Constitution* and/or for a *'Part 2 Enquiry'* under the terms of *the Houses of the Oireachtas (Inquiries, Privileges and Procedures) Act 2013* and that I support and endorse any such initiative on the basis of the evidence contained—or referred to—in the said *Integrity Ireland Report*.

9. That in the interim, and so as to provide for the criteria for continued membership of the United Nations, the Council of Europe and the European Union and so as not to compromise the status of Ireland as a sovereign nation-state nor render it defunct and obsolete due to the proven absences of; (i) the Rule of Law and, (ii) a properly-functioning justice system; I hereby endorse and support the establishment of the *Peoples' Tribunal of Ireland* as per the terms laid out in the provisional 'PTI Mission Statement' in additional context of the 21-page *I-I Declaration* accompanying; to continue in open collaboration and cooperation with lawfully-established

and properly-functioning institutions of the Irish State, until such time as the proper establishment of an authentic justice system complete with lawful, competent and independent Courts.

10. That if I am aware of any *lawful* objections or impediments to the immediate establishment of the *Peoples' Tribunal of Ireland* – complete with the authorities, powers and jurisdictions as laid out in the said PTI Mission Statement – that I will formally advise and inform the record of any such lawful impediments before close of business on or before July 7th 2020 complete with my own proposals (as an incumbent office holder) as to how to address the current absence of the Rule of Law in this State, and I undertake to return the same in writing to the PTI Executive or, that I surrender the opportunity to do so according to the legal principle, *"qui tacet consentire videtur"* – (silence implies consent).

Print Name:_____

Office / Position:_____

Signed:_____Date:_____

Official Stamp Here

Inasmuch as there were no official responses or acknowledgements to the formal legal service of these 'QTC' Notices & Declarations on the respective Irish officials and office holders; then their consent is assumed, and legal authority is conveyed according to the 'qui tacet consentit videtur' legal principle.

This letter to the Chief Justice in May 2020 qualifies as a foundation document; (i) in the Petition to the Houses of the Oireachtas; (ii) accompanying formal approaches to the UN, the CoE and the EU, and (iii) regarding the necessary establishment of *The Peoples Tribunal of Ireland,* inasmuch as this letter further documents the ever-more ridiculous stand-off between one determined, law-abiding citizen and a so-called 'Irish justice system' that is increasingly paralyzed by its own serial duplicities, mendacities, hypocrisies, and cover-ups and frauds.

FORMAL NOTICE & ADVISORY & REQUEST FOR DIRECT INTERVENTION

Dear Mr Clarke / Frank / Sir;

Previous correspondence refers. We write to you (yet again) in your role as, (i) Chief Justice of Ireland in context of the fact that you are also, (ii) a member of the Council of State; (iii) a member of the Presidential Commission; (iv) the Chairperson of the Courts Service Board; (v) the President of the Supreme Court; and (vi) the senior member of the newly-established Judicial Council where you hold the various positions of; (vii) Chairperson of the Board; & (viii) Head of Judicial Conduct Committee; and where you have the primary responsibility for nominating and assigning judges to other positions, committees and boards within the Judicial Council such as, (ix) the Judicial Studies Committee and, (x) the Personal Injuries Guidelines Committee.

You are also a resident of this State, a citizen of the EU and a signatory to the Judge's Constitutional Oath of Office which not only renders you personally 'subject to the law and the Constitution' but that you are likewise bound by a stringent moral, ethical and professional code of conduct.

Notwithstanding your undoubtedly busy schedule Sir, and with due regard to any particular difficulties caused by the Covid-19 pandemic, we write again to draw your explicit, specific attention to several unanswered and unacknowledged letters and Notices dating back to June of last year and including our latest of March 2nd last which, despite being served "Under Seal" on yourself and all of the Justices of the Supreme Court, on the Minister for Justice and on several other senior officials and office holders, has not resulted in any acknowledgements or responses whatsoever.

Similarly, our valid applications for criminal summonses in the CCJ as against a number of senior officials and office holders (including named judges) seems to have been indefinitely (and again, unlawfully) shelved? In short, that we continue to be unlawfully stonewalled by persons who are obliged to act, under statute, to evidence, proofs and knowledge of serious, repeat criminal activity.

In respect of the new Judicial Council and any anticipated attempts to redirect existing complaints and allegations of grave judicial misconduct away from pre-existing statutory and constitutional remedies, we note that *S.89 of the Judicial Council*

Act states; *"Nothing in this Act shall be construed as affecting the operation of section 4 of Article 35 of the Constitution"* — thereby preserving the constitutional right to apply for judicial impeachment directly to the Houses of the Oireachtas.

Neither are there any prohibitions on the lodging of formal criminal complaints with the statutory authorities, nor for applications for criminal summonses under *S.10 of the Petty Sessions (Ireland) Act 1851*. In short, that whatever powers and remedies that may rest with the Judicial Council in future in whatever *authentic* attempts that may be made to curtail gross professional misconduct (and worse) by sitting judges, that any such powers do NOT replace *Article 35.4 of the Constitution*, nor affect the right of the individual to lodge criminal complaints with An Garda Síochána and/or to apply directly for criminal summonses under *S.10 of the Petty Sessions Act*. Accordingly Mr Clarke, this somewhat pitiful tactic of stonewalling / time-wasting / and blockading me (and several others of my acquaintance) from accessing justice is not only legally redundant, but it constitutes in fact, a direct denial of the Rule of Law — which is an inviolable right that we are constitutionally entitled to.

Given that those various aforesaid Notices, Advisories and Formal Declarations provided you and your colleagues with specific, detailed proofs of serious criminal activity ongoing in the Courts; and given that we have documented the same in numerous advisories to the authorities; in criminal complaints to An Garda Síochána; and in affidavits 'on the record' in the Superior Courts; and given we have now exhausted all lawful domestic remedies in seeking the due and proper application of the Rule of Law; we hereby repeat the questions (A, B & C below) outstanding from previous correspondence which we (again) direct to you personally and specifically as the incumbent Office Holder of *the* preeminent Legal Authority in this State, reminding you again Mr Clarke, and most seriously and emphatically, that in circumstances where the State fails and refuses to simply afford us our fundamental rights under EU and International Law, that it then becomes the constitutional duty and moral obligation of the citizen to directly source those rights through alternative means.

A. You have been given all of the facts, details and evidence of a serious criminal fraud being perpetrated on the Courts through the collusive, unlawful actions of various 'Officers of the Court'. My JR case 2017/798 has now been placed 'in legal limbo' through this deliberate fraud and through the subsequent ongoing failures and refusals of ALL of the Irish statutory authorities approached – including the Superior Courts – to properly deal with the matter.

Q: How can I possibly advance my case without participating in this unlawful fraud?

B. The terms of *S.10 of the Petty Sessions (Ireland) Act 1851* provide for 'any person' to apply for and initiate criminal prosecutions as against 'any other person'. This has been specifically endorsed by the High Court, the Court of Appeal and the Supreme Court in recent years.

Q: Why have multiple such valid applications been unlawfully ignored / denied / refused / suppressed or 'disappeared' by over a dozen District Court Judges, and why are our Superior Courts, senior judges and the Minister for Justice all repeatedly failing or refusing to act in face of multiple explicit complaints of serious judicial and DPP prosecutorial misconduct?

C. You have been advised several times now that all of the so-called 'statutory authorities' in this State are (generally speaking – and in the experience of thousands of our members) no more and no less than smoke-and-mirrors operations involved in systemic obstructionism and deception, whose primary agenda is to protect a largely corrupt status quo and NOT actually to 'deliver justice' to the people, as each has so disingenuously stated 'on paper'.

Q: Please identify THE supreme authority in this State to whom we should now turn to in respect of; (i) ongoing legal matters; (ii) the interpretation and application of EU law; and (iii) concerning repeat, criminal failures by the organs of the Irish State (including the Superior Courts) to respect our fundamental human rights regarding access to justice?

An important point needs to be made here. Surely Sir, with all of the legal talent and expertise at your disposal, it should be no big stretch of the imagination that someone up there should, by now, have worked out the inescapable fact; that the longer this asinine stonewalling nonsense goes on, and the longer the list of known accomplices, of co-conspirators and of aiders-and-abettors in these repressive acts, then the sooner the great big lie will be exposed: That we do NOT have a functioning justice system at all, but rather, just the *pretence* of justice; a taxpayer-funded monopoly of so-called 'legal professionals' apathetic, devious and/or sinister as the case may be, comprising a cabal of politically-connected miscreants appointed to High Office where the organs of the State are being hijacked so as to service iniquitous and disreputable ends. This, Mr Clarke, will be your enduring legacy if you do not seize the moment and act without delay, according to law and to conscience.

Naturally Sir, and in respect of these troubling circumstances, any failure to respond—and respond properly without equivocation—within 7 days will be taken as a refusal, and we will act accordingly without further recourse to you. Awaiting your qualified response, and trusting the position is clear.

Yours,

Dr Stephen Manning (etc)

A member of *Integrity Ireland* and Independent candidate for Co. Mayo.

THE PEOPLES TRIBUNAL
of IRELAND

INDEPENDENCE, IMPARTIALITY, INTEGRITY

*MISSION STATEMENT

(i) *The Peoples Tribunal of Ireland* **is an initiative by residents and citizens of the Irish State;** to lawfully address persistent, widespread, endemic lapses and failures of the Irish State to adhere to the Rule of Law in respect of fundamental human rights, and in particular to provide for the individual's right to access justice.

(ii) **To provide for the impartial and objective assessment** and/or investigation of issues, events, actions, questions, enquiries and/or cases which are pertinent to the constitutional integrity of Irish society and to the lawful status of sovereign Irish people.

(iii) **To provide some manner of authoritative, documented redress** for aggrieved citizens/residents which is; (a) honest, fair, objective and impartial; (b) that is independent of government and vested interests; and (c) which is constructed and composed in express alignment with internationally-recognised human rights law, and with EU and domestic law, in strict order of legal precedence according to existing positive law.

(iv) **To aid in the determination of legal certainty** by providing for the production and publication of qualified written mandates in the form of PTI Judicial Orders, Rulings, Findings Directives and/or Decrees to be binding on the parties served, according to the Rule of Law.

(v) **To provide for a People's Prosecution Service** in support of the individual's right to initiate and prosecute criminal proceedings in the Irish Courts under *S.10 of the Petty Sessions (Ireland) Act 1851* and to provide for the active and effective implementation of existing citizens' arrest powers as laid out under *S.4 of the Criminal Law Act 1997*.

(vi) **To provide for independent, qualified arbitration and mediation services.**

(vii) **To provide an open public forum** for residents, citizens and all interested parties to contribute to and learn from the collective experience and expertise of the PTI Membership, in open collaboration with any and all other relevant, pertinent or applicable sources, resources, groups or institutions – whether statutory, private and/or independent – for the purposes outlined herein.

All, as subject to amendment by the PTI Council.*

FOUNDATION DOCUMENTS FOR THE FORMAL ESTABLISHMENT OF THE PTI INCLUDE

- *"The Peoples Tribunal of Ireland Handbook v 1, 2020" ISBN 978-1-906628-89-5*
- *"Criminality in the Irish Courts – and the absence of the Rule of Law" ISBN 978-1-906628-88-8*
- *"Indictment & Application for a Public Enquiry into State-sponsored Criminality" ISBN 978-1-906628-93-2*

And all of the legislation and law as referenced in these combined publications.

www.ingramcontent.com/pod-product-compliance
Lightning Source LLC
Chambersburg PA
CBHW060514280326
41933CB00014B/2964